Immortal Bear
The Stoutest Polar Ship

About the Book

A gallant ship, like a gallant person, seems to have a heart that wins affection and respect. This was true of the *Bear,* which made history at both the top and the bottom of the world. Generations of sailing men knew her as the stoutest ship afloat in the wild seas and grinding ice of the Arctic and Antarctic. Authors Robert H. Rankin and H. R. Kaplan tell her matchless story compellingly from her birth in a Scottish shipyard nearly a century ago, through her long years as a Coast Guard cutter on the Alaskan coast, and as Admiral Byrd's beloved ship on his second expedition to the Antarctic. Is she still alive?

The *Bear* as she first appeared. This photo was taken during her voyage to rescue the Greely Expedition.

Immortal
BEAR

The Stoutest
Polar Ship

by Robert H. Rankin
and H. R. Kaplan

G. P. Putnam's Sons
New York

Contents

Acknowledgments **6**

1 The Curtain Rises **7**

2 First Voyages North **11**

3 Prelude to Fame **27**

4 The Enforcer **41**

5 Mike Healy—The Man and the Legend **51**

6 The *Bear* Against the Arctic **67**

7 The Old Order Changes **97**

8 To the Bottom of the World **118**

9 A Warrior Ship Stands Guard **143**

10 Rest in Peace **153**

Bibliography **156**

Index **158**

Acknowledgments

Many people have cooperated with the authors in making this book possible.

Among those to whom special thanks are due are Dr. Hope K. Holdcamper, Legislative, Judicial and Diplomatic Records Division, National Archives; Miss Elizabeth K. Segedi, photo editor, Headquarters U.S. Coast Guard; Father Vincent I. Bellwoar, SJ, archivist, Georgetown University; Mr. Walter V. Barbash, Audio-Visual Branch, National Archives; Captain Albert A. Heckman USCG, deputy chief, Office of Public and International Affairs, Headquarters, U.S. Coast Guard.

Mrs. Cora B. Ford and Miss Jennifer Suko gave material assistance.

Captain Alfred M. Shaw, Shaw Steamship Company, Ltd., of Halifax, Nova Scotia, former owner of the *Bear* patiently answered many questions and furnished many productive leads to research materials.

Mr. John G. Richards, president of Potomac Arms, Alexandria, Virginia, made many valuable suggestions which were incorporated in the manuscript. Mr. W. B. Greenwood, Mr. Fred Meigs, and Miss Laura Carpenter, of the Navy Department Library, were most helpful in supplying research materials.

1

The Curtain Rises

She was born in 1873, in the shipyard of the old firm of Alexander Stephen and Son at Dundee, Scotland. The company which sired the *Bear* had behind it generations of shipbuilding experience. It built good, honest ships, mostly for the northern sealing trade. Over the years it had learned that of all the environmental enemies men must face, none is more savage or powerful than the sea.

On the whole it had been quite successful in meeting the assault of this ancient enemy. But even so, there were a few dark chapters. No matter how carefully and sturdily a ship was built, you could never foretell the effect of the terrible forces which would be arrayed against her. Ice fields and huge floating ice islands could crush the hulls of even powerfully built ships like eggshells. In fact, the waters into which the sealers ventured were among the most dangerous in all the world.

The wealth represented by seals was often purchased by human blood. In the treacherous waters off the Grand Banks of Newfoundland, dense fog could shroud the vessel completely. Terrible storms could blow up at any time and vent their fury on a luckless vessel. Sailors in the sealing fleet knew that many ships had gone out, never to return. Once you entered that domain of endless sky and water, you were beyond human help.

Knowing this, Stephen of Linthouse, as the firm was sometimes known, took every precaution known to shipbuilders of that time to build good ships. That meant that every nail, every timber, every piece of equipment, no matter how minute, had to be installed with careful precision. There could be no allowance for any areas of weakness. For the company, shipbuilding was more than a business. It was a trust.

At the time of the launching of the *Bear*, in 1873, Stephen of Linthouse had won an honored place in the shipbuilding industry. The virtues which its staff brought to their calling were peculiarly Scots: intelligence, skill, integrity.

When the *Bear*'s prospective owners, Walter Grieve and Company, commissioned the Stephen Company to build the *Bear*, they wanted much more than an ordinary ship. This was to be a vessel which would take advantage of all the sailing lore acquired from generations of sailing experience. Time had shown, for example, that wood rather than iron was preferable for the sealing business. Wood had the strength and resilience to take the battering of northern seas without losing its shape. Iron, on the other hand, which had been used in earlier ships, had proved too brittle. Cold water tended to make the metal even less able to withstand heavy ice pressures. Stephen of Linthouse knew this and was determined to build the toughest wooden ship ever to sail in the sealing trade.

By 1873 most ships were no longer operating solely by sail but were also using steam engines. Shipbuilding had not yet become an engineering science, however. It was still regarded as an art. Like artists, the Stephen shipbuilders poured all their painfully acquired knowledge into the process, as well as their considerable intuition. Since wood was essential to its business, the Stephen company maintained a fleet of its own, which it dispatched to far-off places for especially durable oak, to Norway for pine, and to Burma for teak. It also used Australian iron bark, the toughest wood known. All these materials went into the construction of the sealer *Bear*.

With great care, the builders took oak planks six inches thick and curved them to the outside of the ribs of Swedish iron. The *Bear's* interior was crossed with stanchions and beams and bulkheads, bracing her hull and dividing her into compartments. That very tough wood teak was used for the *Bear's* decks. Because every delay in building meant money lost in trade, Walter Grieve and Company, her owners, were anxious to get her into service as quickly as possible. The 1874 seal hunt was not far off. To meet the schedule, workmen had been operating at top speed. They worked from sunup to sundown and sometimes beyond. Only on the Sabbath did they pause in their labors. The strict Scots' law did not permit work on that day.

In the months after the laying of the keel, swarms of workmen went about their work of bolting steel bedplates to ribs and keel. They put in a good Scots boiler and secured an engine in place. Sailmakers busily cut patterns. Riggers prepared the standing gear to support the masts and the running rigging which would help the engine to propel the *Bear*. Seams in the deck and hull were tightly calked with oakum, smoothly tarred outside. Australian iron bark sheathed the *Bear*'s sides above and below the waterline. To protect her from sea worms and fouling marine life, her bottom was covered with yellow pine and with antifouling mixture. A steel stem plate was fitted onto her solid oak bow, and many coats of paint and varnish were applied to protect the vessel from rust and soakage. Swiftly, the weeks and months passed, and by the end of 1873 the *Bear* was well on the way to completion.

2

First Voyages North

On a bitterly cold day in the winter of 1874 the *Bear* was ready for launching. In the town of Dundee the birth of a new ship was a festive occasion. Throughout the shipyard and the community a holiday spirit prevailed. The townsfolk were so anxious to watch the launching that they were willing to pay for admission for the privilege of being in the shipyard. Proceeds were to be donated to charity.

Gathered on a small platform of the bow were the new owners, the officials of Walter Grieve and Company, and their families, as well as Alexander Stephen and his son, William. Conversation was gay and animated, but there was underlying concern. Failure to achieve a successful launching was considered bad luck. Crews would be reluctant to sail on her, and her prospects were not considered bright. If the traditional bottle of champagne did not smash against the *Bear's* side, that, too, was bad luck. And if the new vessel did not hit the water cleanly, full on and upright, old salts believed the ship would eventually run into disaster.

After what seemed an eternity to the people on the deck, the foreman raised his hand and gave the signal for the launching. A silence descended on the group as a lady chosen for the ceremony stepped forward. Firmly she grasped the bottle of champagne suspended by a ribbon. As the *Bear* began to slide slowly toward the water at the foreman's command, she drew back the bottle and smashed it against the figurehead of the small polar bear with forepaws uplifted. There were cheers when the bottle broke cleanly and the wine ran down the side of the newly christened ship. Gathering speed, the *Bear* made a perfect launch in the Tay River. Her story had begun.

The new shipowners had pressing economic worries. Much of their capital was invested in the new sealer, and they could not afford to miss the sealing season of 1874. While the launching had dispelled some of their worry, there was still work to be done before the *Bear* could begin earning money for them. At the Dundee dock, workmen raced to complete her fitting out. They installed her fore and mizzenmasts, and under each one they put three shillings. The coins were placed heads up for luck. According to the ancient lore of the sea, the money was to serve as payment for the grim boatman

Charon and his crew, who ferried the dead across the River Styx.

The new vessel was to be a steam barkentine—that is, a three-masted vessel with a steam engine propulsion plant in addition to sail. Highly skilled workmen prepared her complicated rigging. Simultaneously mechanics in the engine and fireroom adjusted bearings, tightened steam and water lines, and tested them under pressure. At last they were satisfied the *Bear* was ready for her sea trial.

For her first real taste of salt water, the *Bear* headed for the North Sea. Those choppy, dangerous waters would test her mettle to the full. The *Bear*'s performance soon allayed any doubts of her seaworthiness. She met the challenge of wind and wave like a veteran.

For her first skipper, the *Bear* was assigned Alexander Graham, a hardy Scots sailor and one of the best in the Grieve fishing fleet. He was a veteran of the trade and well qualified to pass judgment on the *Bear*. About a month after her launching the *Bear* was on her way from Greenock, Scotland, to the center of the seal fisheries off St. John's, Newfoundland.

Captain Graham was quickly aware that he had an exceptional ship under him. She was not a large ship by modern standards—about 198 feet long and nearly 30 feet in the beam. Although the *Bear* was not an icebreaker, her unusually heavy oak framing and planking and her iron-bark sheathing were hardy enough to carry

Another view of the *Bear* as she originally appeared. This photo was taken shortly after the *Bear* was purchased by the U.S. Navy.

her through situations which would have crushed a more lightly built vessel. There was no question that the *Bear* was a masterpiece of the shipbuilder's art and a tribute to the skill of the Stephens shipyard.

Besides being sturdy, Graham found that the *Bear* was remarkably self-sustaining, with a good capacity for coal, water, and supplies. This, together with her simple and dependable power plant and adequate sail, enabled her to stay at sea for lengthy periods. Her speed was rather slow, averaging about eight knots, but in an emergency she could crowd on another couple of knots. She had been designed for durability rather than speed.

Today's sailors would have found living conditions on the *Bear* primitive. But she rode comfortably in heavy weather, and the men on board thought her a good home afloat. Ventilation was poor in the crew's quarters. These, however, were sailors of another age and accustomed to the discomforts of a seafaring life. Another reason for putting up with some of the *Bear*'s shortcomings was her growing identity. The men began to have a feeling of affection and loyalty for the ship. Later, her sailors would proudly tell other seafaring men, "I'm from the *Bear*."

Graham pushed the *Bear* hard to arrive at the sealing grounds on time. Unless she reached St. John's within the next two weeks, he could miss out on the best of the seal catch. By now the bulk of the sealing fleet had assembled in the harbor of St. John's, impatiently waiting to start their annual seal hunt.

As the *Bear* approached Newfoundland, she ran into an area of huge floating ice mountains. Each year these islands of ice move south from the Arctic, calving off the Greenland glaciers. Through passing vessels which displayed the signal flags of the Ice Code, she received the latest information on the location of the bergs.

Older hands on the *Bear* were soon telling younger crew members of the white haze, or ice blink, in the direction of Newfoundland. This denoted the presence of the ice pack. Immediately ahead, the haze was a bluish white, indicating ice and water, while darker water blink in the distance came from the open sea.

The young sailors also learned about the harshness of the Arctic winter, which freezes the northern waters to a far depth. Then, through the constant action of wind and wave, the ice is broken into large fragments, known as floes. They heard, too, of the Labrador Current into which Greenland's 20 major glaciers calve off an unceasing number of white monsters or icebergs. In a normal ice year about 400 of these behemoths of the deep come down into North Atlantic shipping lanes, constituting a serious hazard to men and ships. The bergs had already brought disaster to many a good ship and its crew and would continue to do so until the fateful evening of April 12, 1912, when the greatest liner of her time, the White Star ship *Titanic*, struck an iceberg and went down near Newfoundland with more than 1,500 persons. That led to the establishment of the International Ice Patrol, which since 1914 has kept a constant vigil for icebergs in North Atlantic shipping lanes. The patrol has kept the loss of men and ships to a minimum.

In 1874, however, there was no patrol, and all that the skipper had to go by was the information he received from passing ships. This was often inadequate and did not accurately reflect the current ice situation.

The warm Labrador Current served another purpose besides carrying icebergs into sea lanes. It brought an enormous quantity of marine life upon which various species of sea animals lived. The approximate route of the current is down from the polar sea through the islands north of Newfoundland. Other portions of the current flow through Robeson Channel, Kennedy Channel, Kane Basin, Smith Sound, and along the western shores of Baffin Bay in a southerly direction.

The great mass of sea life brought down by the Labrador Current reaches its peak near the Grand Banks of Newfoundland. It is in this great feeding ground that fish, as well as seals are to be found in immense numbers. As regularly as though signaled by some biological clock, the seals arrive in the hundreds of thousands. From October through the winter they gorge themselves on fish. Then, as spring approaches, they begin their annual trek to the north. Timed by the same biological clock, the female seals begin to calve their young early in March. Warned by the same instinct, the females avoid the land areas and look for an ice floe on which to have their young.

For long periods the seals swim in a northerly direction, looking for the ice pack. As they swim, they frolic in the open waters until at last the mother seal finds an ice floe and prepares to bear her young. Newfoundlanders know that February 28 is the literal "birthday" for the harp seals. Nearly all the young whitecoats are born at that time. The baby hoods are almost always found farther at sea than the harps. They are born approximately March 5.

For a month the mother seals ride their ice floes, leaving them only to find food for the baby seals. They are exceptionally devoted parents and always return to the floes to nurse their offspring.

By March 15 the sealing season has started in earnest. The young harps by this time have attained a weight of around 40 pounds. In another two weeks they will be strong enough to swim north and out of reach of the hunters. That is why the sealers in St. John's Harbor were so anxious to get started. The time in which they had to make their catch was so limited that every day lost was an economic disaster.

The seals hunted with such ferocity each year in the North Atlantic were not like their sleek counterparts in the North Pacific. They were covered with thick, oily hair and were hunted for the oil distilled from their fat, serving as a base for perfumes and illumination. The skins were used in the manufacture of patent leather, then much favored by dandies for footwear. Two great seal herds were principally involved; the harps, so called because of a peculiar harp-shaped marking on their backs, and the hoods, whose skulls were covered by a hoodlike cowl of fur.

The trade on which the *Bear* was embarked was not new. It had been going on since early in the seventeenth century. In those far-off days, whalers hunting on the borders of the Arctic also sought the seals for their skins, blubber, and tusks, the latter providing a somewhat inferior ivory. The seals' teeth were also bought from the natives. At the height of the whaling industry the hunters tended to overlook the seals, preferring the more profitable whales. But with the advent of the Industrial Revolution, commercial interest turned once again to the seals.

Each fall, with unfailing regularity, the Atlantic seal herds head south from Baffin Bay, far to the north of St. John's. The harps go past the Labrador coast, while the hoods swim past Greenland. Then they continue on to the Grand Banks and other fishing grounds. There they settle down for the winter to feed and grow fat. With the approach of spring the seals move north to meet the pack. The baby hoods, always found to seaward of the harps, are a blue-gray color when born.

By the time the *Bear* reached St. John's, the sealing fleet was preparing to head out on the seal hunt. There was little evidence of spring, but every sealer, or swiler, as they were popularly known, knew he had about two weeks in which to make his catch. The milk-fed whitecoats at the time weighed about 40 pounds. With each day they were gaining in strength and the ability to survive. Soon they would be able to swim until they disappeared in the vast northern sea. So it was a race against time.

In mid-March the armada of ships in the North Atlantic sealing trade set sail for the treacherous northern waters. The farther northward they pushed, the greater the risks became. Year after year brought its toll. Eager to amass the largest possible catch, the hunters sailed into dangerous ice fields. Sometimes a vessel would be caught in a giant vise between two ice floes capable of crushing its sides like an eggshell. Against the silent, unremitting hostility of the Arctic, the sealers seemed pathetically inadequate.

As the ships sailed on, the rivalry, which had been good natured at first, began to take on a sharper edge.

It took strong hands to hold the *Bear*'s wheel as the floes crunched against her rudder. The careful workmanship of the Dundee shipyard began to pay off as the *Bear* cut through floes with her steel-shod bow, moving swiftly through open leads and ramming into ice six feet thick. At last a few seals were sighted in the distance. Every man on board could feel the tension rise in him as he prepared his gear for what lay ahead. In spite of their heavy clothing, which included several suits of underwear, in addition to ice goggles and mittens, they felt a slight inward chill.

The razor-sharp sculping knife was whetted to even more deadly sharpness, and all eyes strained for the first sight of massed seals. Then it happened. Straight ahead, stretching endlessly before them, was a great seal herd. They could hear the peculiar cry of the whitecoats in the cold air. Their faith in the *Bear* had been rewarded. She was a lucky ship and had brought them into the very midst of this vast seal herd. In that moment the men loved their ship. Disregarding personal danger, they clambered down her sides to begin the hunt. From floe to floe they jumped in pursuit of the seals, sometimes slipping into the icy water. Sealing was not a pleasant business. Never having seen men before, the young whitecoats had not yet learned the meaning of fear. A hard smash on the head put whitecoat after whitecoat to death. Then a slash of the sculping knife took off the skin and its thick layer of valuable blubber. The hunters fastened the rapidly growing pile of sculps together and they were towed into groups, or pans. The deck of the *Bear* was slippery with the blood of the slaughtered animals as the sealers poured baskets of ice around the bleeding skins to keep the blubber intact.

There was no pause in the gory task. Men killed

until their arms became too tired to lift the heavy sculping knives. The massacre went on from dawn to dark, pausing only briefly when the hunters had a mug of hot tea or other nourishment. The terrible assault soon eliminated all the seals in the vicinity of the ship, and the sealers extended their hunting area farther on the ice. By nightfall the men of the *Bear* had returned to their ship, exhausted but happy in the knowledge they were making a phenomenal kill. This could turn out to be one of the best hunts of their careers. In their anticipation of the good fortune ahead, they forgot their weariness, their dirty, bloodstained faces and clothing, as well as their crowded bunks. At best they could snatch only a few hours' sleep before starting another day of exhausting, bloody, but profitable labor.

For ten days the hapless seals were butchered. The *Bear* was now carrying such a heavy cargo of seals that living space was becoming scarce. Every sealing skipper was anxious to be the first to hoist his flag indicating that his hold was full. It would make him the envy of all other skippers.

Captain Graham was a proud skipper as his ship seeking smaller groups of older and more widely scattered seals. He had virtually exhausted the supply of the more lucrative harps and was now searching for hoods. This later quarry was different from those he had pursued before. Hoods are fighters, and the older seals have enormously strong flippers and viciously sharp teeth. Instead of submitting passively to slaughter, they often prefer to stand and fight. This is especially true when they feel that their young are endangered.

The easy pickings of the earlier part of the hunt were over. These animals could seize the gaff, force it from the hands of the hunter, and start an attack of their own. Because of the increased difficulty of hunting, the catch now was smaller. Many tough old hoods had to be dispatched by rifle fire. The hunt was nearly over, however, but not before the *Bear* had shown her mettle as a sealer. In her first hunt she brought back more than 12,000 sculps, worth about one-fourth of her building cost. Her owners had good cause for rejoicing. This was only the first of many memorable hunts the *Bear* would make.

April brought an end to sealing activity. All hands looked forward to the comforts of a good bed and a home that did not rock under their feet. When they finally made their way up the channel toward St. John's, they were a proud and happy group of men. The fame of their ship had already been spread through the fleet. It would not be difficult to recruit another crew after this catch. As a matter of fact, practically all the same men, except for a few, returned for the next sealing season.

Captain Graham was a proud skipper as his ship made her way up the channel toward St. John's. At the docks the sculps were unloaded, and the sealers drew their pay and went ashore. While lying at anchor, the *Bear*'s crew cleaned and scrubbed the vessel until she no longer had the smell and look of a sealer just returned from the kill.

It was the *Bear*'s destiny to remain a sealer for the next ten years. In that time she would make two voyages under Captain Graham, six under Captain Levi Diamond, and two under Francis Ash. At the moment her future in the sealing trade looked bright. Sailors were convinced that she had been touched by whatever magic makes a lucky ship. No disaster could befall them when they sailed in her.

The climax of the *Bear*'s sealing career came in 1883, when, under the command of Charles Dawe, she achieved the best catch of the season—30,298 skins. She had been able to punch her way through the pack and hit the main herd. This time the seal kill was so huge that even the holds were filled, and the sculps had to be crammed into every other available space. Men who were already living under intolerably crowded conditions had to give up even more of their living quarters to make room for the ever-mounting cargo of skins. When this space was gone, the sealers resorted to dumping their extra coal overboard.

Spurred by the phenomenal success of their voyage, the men cheerfully endured all discomforts. Always before their eyes was the prospect of the money and comfort assured by a record catch. Finally, there was no more room for additional skins. The *Bear*, in the language of the trade was log-loaded, almost bursting with skins. It was a happy skipper who ordered flags hoisted to the mastheads to proclaim the good tidings. When the blast of the foghorn called the men back to the ship, the sight of the flags filled them with jubilation. In their exultation the men began to cheer and sing. To cap it all, the muster of hands on the *Bear's* deck showed that everyone had made it back. The catch had been magnificent, and no lives had been lost.

The *Bear* was the first of the sealing fleet to return to the harbor of St. John's. The share allotted to each swiller was $100, a great sum by the standards of those days.

At the offices of Walter Grieve and Company, there was equal joy. The ship whose launching they had watched with such concern more than a decade before had turned out to be one of the finest sealers ever to enter the trade. Both at St. John's and at Greenock, Scotland, glasses were raised to toast the *Bear*, her skipper and crew.

Like a warrior returning from battle, the *Bear* returned to Greenock for overhaul and repair. When she came back to Newfoundland in February, 1884, she sported a new boiler and a fresh coat of paint. Everything had been attended to, and she was prepared to resume her sealing career.

But unknown to the *Bear* and her crew, fate was to

take a hand in her affairs. To their amazement, the men of the *Bear* found out in St. John's that their great ship had been purchased by the United States Navy. The occasion for the purchase was the marooning of an explorer, Army Lieutenant A. W. Greely, and his party in the Arctic. A tough, dependable ship was needed to smash her way through the ice to the stranded scientists, who were in danger of dying of cold and starvation. So urgent was the need for the *Bear* that the Secretary of the Navy had purchased her before Congress appropriated money for the purpose.

The *Bear* had made her last sealing run. Ahead of her was a new career as a rescue ship in the Arctic. Before that adventure was done, her name would be renowned.

3

Prelude to Fame

The episode that brought fame to the *Bear* and to Lieutenant Adolphus Washington Greely, U.S. Army Signal Corps, was the Lady Franklin Bay Expedition of 1882.

The expedition was one of a long series of attempts by the nations of the world to penetrate the polar regions. For centuries, imaginations had been drawn irresistibly to the vast white areas at the top and bottom of the world. Their interest to the north originally was in finding a northwest passage through the Arctic to the wealth of the Orient. This desire to find that elusive passage became an obsession to explorers of all nations. The record of Arctic exploration was a tragic chronicle of death and frustrated hopes.

Still fresh in the minds of Greely and his contemporaries was the fate of the expedition led by the British explorer Sir John Franklin to the Arctic. In 1845 Franklin was given command of a party of 129 picked men from the Royal Navy and two stout ships, the *Erebus* and *Terror*, which had been tested in previous explorations. He left England on July 16. Two years later, no news had come from his party. In 1847 the British public, alarmed by the complete disappearance of the Franklin Expedition, started to organize relief attempts.

Although the rescue fleets followed the route traveled by Franklin, no trace of him could be found. For ten years, they persevered to find Franklin and his men—but to no avail. Then one of the searchers, Sir John Rae, met a group of Eskimos near Pelly Bay in Victoria Land who provided the first clue to Franklin's fate. In the possession of the Eskimos were silver knives and other objects bearing the initials of Franklin and officers of his command. Despite Rae's findings, there was a general reluctance to accept the grisly verdict. But eventually it was obvious that the entire party had perished. The clinching evidence was found by Sir Francis McClintock in 1859, when he came upon messages scrawled by Franklin in 1848. From these brief bits of writing the world learned that the expedition had been destroyed under the assault of the vicious Arctic winters.

In 1875 a new chapter began in the long and tragic tale of Arctic exploration. A young lieutenant, Karl Weyprecht of the Austro-Hungarian Army, proposed that the nations of the world combine their efforts to set up a string of weather observation stations in the Arctic and Antarctic. Although Weyprecht did not live to see it, his proposal was ultimately adopted at the international polar conferences at Bern, Switzerland, and at Hamburg, Germany. The ten nations at the conference agreed that each should assume responsibility for setting up one or more weather observation posts. These were the events that led to the Greely Expedition.

The United States sent two expeditions to the far north, the most northerly being headed by thirty-seven-year-old Lieutenant Greely. In 1881, Greely's party sailed up Smith Sound and landed at Franklin Bay in August of the same year. The ship that carried him to Lady Franklin Bay in the far northeastern portion of Canada was the *Proteus*. Richard Pike was its master. Chosen because of his long experience in navigating northern waters, Pike accomplished his mission and reported that the Greely party had been brought safely to its destination.

Upon arriving at Lady Franklin Bay, Greely quickly established a station and began a program of observation and exploration. He soon revealed the qualities of strength and character which were to bring him fame and eventual advancement to the rank of major general in the U.S. Army. His diaries, published after the incident, reveal him as a strong, sensitive man, dedicated to duty and to science. He was a graduate of West Point and had fought in the Civil War.

The expedition plan called for a two-year stay in the Arctic. As a precautionary measure, supplies sufficient for a three-year stay were taken. A supply ship was scheduled to visit Greely's station the following year, in 1882, with additional supplies and personnel. In the event that the supply ship could not reach Greely, supplies and provisions were to be cached at Littleton Island and Cape Sabine. Both these points are south of Lady Franklin Bay on Smith Sound, just north of Baffin Bay.

The last phase of the plan entailed the dispatch of another ship in 1883 to pick up the expedition and its equipment for return to the United States. If this became impossible because of the ice, the vessel was to remain in northern waters until it was forced out by the ice. In that case, a relief party was to be sent north by dog sled to meet Greely.

It seemed a reasonably good plan. But things began to go wrong. The first mishap occurred when the supply ship *Neptune* was turned back by heavy ice before reaching Greely at Lady Franklin Bay. Then the *Proteus*, which had been chartered to take the Greely party home, was crushed in the ice and sank off Cape Sabine. The crew and a very small amount of food were saved from the wreck. These meager provisions were deposited at Cape Sabine, and the crew of the *Proteus* made their way back to civilization.

The loss of the *Proteus* was a serious matter. The

Commander Winfield Scott Schley, USN, commanding officer of the expedition which rescued Greely and the other survivors of his Lady Franklin Bay Expedition.

only thing Greely could do now was to abandon his headquarters and travel south by small boats. This plan was predicated on his finding food deposited at points along the way. But there was no food, and the situation of the men became desperate.

There was a rising public indignation at the clumsiness of the efforts to relieve Greely. By 1884 Congress seemed more preoccupied with the cost and feasibility of a rescue than with the survival of Greely and his twenty-four men.

Recognizing the desperate urgency of the situation, Secretary of the Navy William Chandler decided to act. He had been secretly negotiating for the purchase of vessels capable of attempting the rescue. Hearing of the *Bear* and her exploits, he made up his mind to buy her. Accordingly, four days before Congress actually appropriated the money, he purchased her for the bargain price of $100,000. Also purchased for the rescue expedition was the sealer *Thetis*. England kindly made available the exploration vessel *Alert*. A collier, the *Loch Garry*, was chartered to provide coal for the other ships. Aroused by the public clamor, Congress finally offered a reward of $25,000 to anyone discovering the Greely party.

The *Bear* and the other members of the rescue fleet were ordered to the Brooklyn Navy Yard for refitting. Commander Winfield Scott Schley, U.S. Navy, was placed in charge of the expedition, and Lieutenant

William H. Emory, Jr., was ordered to the *Bear* as her first American skipper.

At the yard, the *Bear* was fitted out for a two-year cruise in the far north, and a disciplined Navy crew of thirty-four came aboard her. On March 17, 1884, the British ensign came down, and the Stars and Stripes replaced it. The *Bear* was now a vessel in the U.S. Navy.

Although the *Bear* was in excellent condition and had been recently overhauled, every precaution was taken to make her equal to her task. Under Emory's supervision, the *Bear* was reinforced with additional supports and iron straps. Her machinery and rigging were checked and repaired. Emory also did all he could to make the *Bear* more habitable for her Navy crew. He introduced such refinements as bunks with curtains to afford privacy, and bulkheads were lined with felt to keep out the Arctic cold.

Emory was a prudent officer. He purchased clothing especially designed for the rigors of the north and a variety of canned goods.

On April 24, 1884, the *Bear* steamed out of New York Harbor. In spite of Emory's optimism, matters did not go promisingly for the newly commissioned Navy ship *Bear*. The Arctic was not long in hurling its weapons against the small fleet. One gale was of such force that it tore off the *Bear*'s bridge.

At St. John's Emory took on additional supplies of high-quality coal to give his ship more speed. In anticipation of the final push, he also took on board sleds and dogs from Labrador. Then he continued his push northward.

Three days out of Upernavik, a small Danish settlement on the west coast of Greenland, while steaming near the shore, the *Bear's* crew was startled by a sudden jarring motion of the ship. She had hit a submerged rock. For anxious moments, everyone wondered whether this would be the end of the expedition. But Emory ordered full speed astern, and the vessel broke clear.

On May 13 Emory reached Godhavn, where he waited for three days for a change of wind. Despite his impatience to proceed with the rescue, Emory realized that he could not afford to risk his ship and crew to gales from the south which could force him into the ice.

He took advantage of the opportunity to lay in sixty days' supplies on deck in the event that the ship was hurt by the ice. The spare propeller also was lashed to the deck. The crew practiced fire drills and procedures to abandon ship. In taking these precautions, Emory was aware of the tragic fate of the *Proteus* which could have been averted had similar measures been taken.

Three days later the wind blew from the north while the *Bear* continued to push north. After a few days out, the *Bear* was halted. Around the ship formed a solid mass of ice. Suddenly, on May 27, the ice pack moved offshore, and a lead opened to the north. The *Bear* moved swiftly ahead, taking advantage of the opening. Then, about 20 miles out of Upernavik, Emory's luck ran out temporarily. An ice block had formed. Though Emory scanned the waters in all directions from the crow's nest, no lead appeared anywhere.

There was nothing to do but head back to Upernavik and try again when conditions permitted. It meant that more precious time would be lost.

At Upernavik the *Loch Garry* filled the *Bear*'s coal bunkers. Meanwhile, Emory heard interesting news: Eskimos reported they had seen five white men in the vicinity of Cape York. The cape lies at the northwestern tip of Greenland, just above a particularly treacherous ice-choked body of water known as Melville Bay.

From Upernavik to Cape York was a considerable distance. Both Emory and Commander Schley, leader of the expedition, agreed that once they arrived at the cape, a party would be put over the side to hunt for what remained of Greely's group.

On the afternoon of May 29 the *Bear* and *Thetis* raised anchor and left Upernavik for Cape York. The *Loch Garry* was left behind to wait for the *Alert*. The *Loch Garry* had not been built for heavy duty in the Arctic and would have to be convoyed by the *Alert* later in the season when more leads opened in the ice.

The *Bear* and *Thetis*, making good progress, reached Kingitok by the evening of May 29. For two frustrating days they were locked in the ice before finally being released by strong winds from the southwest. The opening of leads to the north and west now made it possible for the vessels to move a bit farther north. Then passage was once more blocked by ice. This time, however, Emory spotted a lead close to shore and immediately started to move through it. Behind the *Bear* was the *Thetis*, Schley's flagship. The *Bear* was proceeding between two icebergs when her crew was horrified by a sudden jar, accompanied by a terrible screeching sound. Like a wounded animal, the vessel seemed to rear up and hang suspended in the air. Then the tough sealer pulled free. The crew knew what had happened: Their ship had smashed into a rock concealed by the water.

How badly had the *Bear* been damaged by the accident? If it turned out to be extensive, the *Bear's* part in the rescue was ended. But it was found that the damage could be repaired.

The *Bear* and *Thetis* had been drifting northward with the ice pack when open water appeared to the north. Between the ships and the open sea was much heavy ice, however. Doggedly the *Bear* smashed her way through the ice.

In the open sea the *Bear* made up some of the lost time. Four miles short of Cape York she was forced to stop by the ice. But the cape was clearly visible from the deck. The vessel had made the first real breakthrough in the rescue attempt.

The *Bear* was able to reach Cary Island in the middle of Baffin Bay while the *Thetis* sailed on to Littleton

Lieutenant A. W. Greely, USA, leader of the ill-fated Lady Franklin Bay Expedition. This photo was taken about two weeks after his rescue.

Island. At Cary Island was found the record left by the *Proteus* a year earlier. Yet no evidence of Greely's survival could be discovered.

The search now led to Cape Sabine. Through gale winds and a blizzard the ships pushed their search. Boat parties were sent out in all directions to comb nearby islands. The *Bear's* cutter, named the *Cub*, was put under the command of Lieutenant John C. Colwell, who was directed to round the point and search Cape Sabine itself.

On Stalknecht Island crumpled papers were found in a cairn. They contained the first news the searchers had yet found about Greely. These records had originally been left there by Greely's second-in-command, Lieutenant James Booth Lockwood. Dated September 22, 1883, they disclosed that the Greely party had made "camp four and one half miles west of Cape Sabine, food for forty days, 25 men, all well."

All well, indeed! It was now June 21, 1884, and the forty days had long since passed. But the searchers were now hard on the trail of Greely. Schley boarded the *Bear* as she prepared to sail the few remaining miles up the coast while the *Thetis* was left to pick up the landing parties.

Lieutenant Colwell, aboard the *Cub*, was on his way to Cape Sabine. When he and his party reached the cape, they climbed a steep slope. At the summit they shouted. Incredibly they heard a faint human cry in reply. Not far off they found an emaciated, sick man, so weak with hunger he could scarcely hold aloft an oar with signal rags tied to it. He was Private Francis Long, one of Greely's party.

Only seven had survived out of the original party of twenty-five. Almost dead from his ordeal, Private Long was carried back to the *Bear* while Colwell ran on to a sagging tent on a slightly elevated piece of ground. The tent was blackened by smoke, and the Arctic wind was blowing its flaps wildly. He peered into the tent and saw five creatures resembling corpses. Greely himself was on his hands and knees looking through the entrance. He looked less than human with his long beard and hair, face and hands grimed with the dirt of many months. Not far away lay Corporal Joseph Elison. His nose, hands, and feet had been frozen. Next to him was Private Maurice Connell, his body as cold as a corpse.

Colwell and his men provided hot liquids and such bits of food as the starved men could digest without danger. Tenderly the sailors picked up the broken men and carried them on board the rescue ships.

The *Bear*'s crew began collecting Greely's records and equipment. What they saw was a scene that would remain with them as long as they lived. On that desolate cape, snow and ice filled every hollow. Not far from the hut a dead man had been laid out on a rock slab. His woolen cap was over his face, and his hands had been crossed on his breast in the classic attitude of death. His clothing and blankets were fastened around his body with straps and bits of rope. He was Private Roderick R. Schneider, the last to die, and the others had been too weak to bury him.

Farther up the cape the rescue party found a burial ground where other bodies lay in a row, covered with moss and rocks. The first of the graves was marked by a decent cross. The others became increasingly shallow, testifying eloquently to the growing weakness of the survivors. The corpses of five other men had been placed in a hole in shore ice where they were washed to sea and lost forever.

As the survivors of Greely's party gained in strength, details of their ordeal became known. When the *Proteus* failed to arrive on schedule, Greely and his men realized that they would have to face the onslaught of an Arctic winter without sufficient food or clothing. Soon weeks of hunger, sickness, and cold began to take their toll.

As supplies dwindled, the party was reduced to eating moss, which brought on violent attacks of diarrhea. They ate the dirty oil-tanned covering of Greely's sleeping bag, which, as he recorded in his diary, "was very repugnant to us." One by one, the members of the party succumbed to the inhuman hardships.

From a respected but generally unknown sealing ship, the *Bear* had become a vessel of international renown. The accomplishment of the Greely rescue represented one of the high points of her career. But the greater part of her long voyage still lay ahead of her. And before the story was done, there would be some surprising twists.

4

The Enforcer

When the *Bear* returned from her successful rescue mission in 1884, she was world-famous. She and her crew were given heroes' welcomes. At the New York Navy Yard, where she was docked on her return, visitors thronged on board to look at the renowned ship. Yet, ironically, at the height of her fame, the United States Navy declared her unfit for further service. She was placed out of commission for the purpose of selling her out of the service. It seemed a wry twist to a heroic story.

As it turned out, the Navy was not being ungrateful. The act of Congress under which the *Bear* had been bought made it clear that she was to be sold as soon as the Greely Relief Expedition was completed. Also, wooden ships were passing from the naval scene. By modern standards, the *Bear* appeared no longer suitable for naval use.

But to the credit of the Revenue Cutter Service, later the U.S. Coast Guard, it knew a good ship when it saw one. Recognizing in the *Bear* the sturdy, seagoing qualities so essential to its work, the service negotiated with the Navy for the *Bear*'s transfer. By act of Congress, dated March 3, 1885, with the concurrence of the Navy, the *Bear* was transferred to the Treasury Department for use in Alaskan waters and the Arctic Ocean. The valiant warrior of the northland would continue to work in its icy waters. Again, fate had determined that the *Bear*'s days of service were far from over. In fact, the greater part of her work still lay ahead.

Taking possession of the *Bear* for the Revenue Cutter Service was Captain Alvin A. Fengar. On March 3, 1885, a new pennant took the breeze from her main truck, the ensign of the Revenue Cutter Service. She was to carry it for the next forty years on patrol, the longest time ever spent on that duty by any ship in the history of the service.

The *Bear* was entering a service rich in naval history. Ships of the Revenue Cutter Service had played an important role in the conflict with the British in the War of 1812 and had subsequently taken part in the Seminole War, the Mexican War of 1848, and the Civil War. Primarily, however, the mission of the service was humane: to come to the help of distressed vessels and mariners without regard to nationality or political differences. This

remains one of the major missions of the U.S. Coast
Guard.

The operation of which the *Bear* became a part in 1885
—the Bering Sea Patrol, now known as the Alaskan Patrol—had been in existence since 1867, when the United
States acquired Alaska from Russia.

On November 8, 1885, the *Bear* steamed out of Staten
Island, New York, and headed for San Francisco by way
of Cape Horn. On February 23, 1886, she reached San
Francisco, where the *Bear*'s captain, A. B. Davis, turned
over his command to Captain Mike Healy. The *Bear,
Rush,* and *Corwin* made up what was then called the
Bearing Sea Patrol. In the next forty years the *Bear*
would carry out search and rescue missions, pursue
fugitives, transport government officials to their posts,
protect the seal herds, feed the Eskimos, supply them
with medicines, and serve as a floating court of justice.
During those early days of the territory, captains of
cutters on the patrol were virtually the only representatives of law and order. They had to supply a rough-and-
ready sort of justice, with no time for all the niceties of
legal procedure.

Nearly all of the white settlements in Alaska's early
years as a territory were concentrated in the southeastern
portion, with only a few traders and adventurers to the
north. It was in the more thickly settled southeastern part
of the territory that the greatest protection was needed
against Indians. In the first ten years of American occu-

pation the federal government was represented by a few scattered garrisons. When the Army left in 1877, the ships of the Revenue Cutter Service took over the job of law enforcement in the vast Alaskan Territory.

After the *Bear* left San Francisco to take up her patrol duties, she sailed to Sitka. Many problems lay ahead of her. Not the least of these was keeping liquor from Indians and Eskimos, who had acquired an inordinate craving for it during the Army occupation. Although Congress by the act of July 27, 1868, had tried to bar the sale of liquor to the Indians, the Indians circumvented the law by making it themselves. They had been taught the secret of liquor distilling by the soldiers. While under the influence of the raw liquor Eskimos and Indians became belligerent, engaging in frequent fights with equally drunken whites. It was a classic example of the corrupting effect of the white man's civilization on a primitive people.

Enforcement of law and order among the territory's population was by no means the only problem facing the *Bear*. Withdrawal of the Russians from the rich fishing and sealing grounds had created a huge vacuum into which adventurers poured from all over the world. The prize for which they contended was the handsome and valuable Alaskan fur seal, highly prized in the fashion marts of the world. Eager to obtain as many skins as possible before the authorities clamped down, the hunters started to annihilate the seal herds. Not only were

During the *Bear's* long voyages into Alaskan waters the crew often amused itself with a ship's mascot—a real bear. This one was photographed aboard the cutter in the 1920's with bandaged head and crutch.

Cutter Bear's Mascot

they destroying the herds, but they were also bringing death to the natives. The Aleuts, who inhabited the sealing areas and who normally worked during the summer catching and curing fish for the winter food supply, were persuaded to go sealing instead. Some companies paid in food; others in liquor. It was a shocking example of human greed.

It was recommended that the islands be made a fed-

45

eral reservation to protect both the islanders and the seals. The recommendation was put into effect in 1870, and for a while the cutthroat scramble for sealing profits was halted. As a further precaution the government leased the sealing privilege to a single concern, the Alaska Commercial Company; established regulations for the killing of seals on the islands; made provision for the Aleuts' welfare; and assigned an agent to hold the company to the contract. It now became the cutters' responsibility to protect the herd from interlopers.

For a while it looked as though the government had solved the problem. But there was one drawback. Seals follow their instincts without regard for international law. How could you prevent seals from migrating from their haven to the open sea? The fur seal is a migratory creature, and its behavior pattern is cyclic and predictable. Treaties, however well intentioned, could not alter this basic fact of nature.

In their migrations the seals traveled hundeds of miles into the open sea in search of herring and cod. At the time that the *Bear* entered the waters of the territory, seals were being destroyed at a sickening rate in the open sea. Known as pelagic sealing, the practice threatened to decimate the seal herds.

The crime of hunting seals in the open sea was that the hunters killed anything within sight, without distinguishing between males or females, pups or bachelor seals.

During an extensive Congressional investigation of the

Another view of the *Bear* in northern waters.

sordid situation, hunters told of great numbers of dead pups washed up on the bleak shores of the spawning grounds. Their mothers had been butchered by the hunters, eager for the valuable skins. By the mid-1890's the seal herd was on the verge of extinction. The matter had reached the proportions of a national scandal. So brutal and indiscriminate were the killings that outraged men and women wrote letters to editors protesting the inhuman practice. Public pressure was slowly building up for strong governmental action.

In 1890 the United States declared the Bering Sea under American jurisdiction. This meant that law enforcement in that area was primarily a U.S.-responsibility. Then in 1891 the United States and British governments worked out an agreement under which the Royal Navy undertook to help protect seals from British poachers. Further measures were taken in 1894 and in 1897 to extend the zone within which American ships were prohibited from catching seals. To help tighten the surveillance, the Revenue Cutter Service in 1895 sent additional cutters north to make up the Bering Sea Patrol.

All these measures helped, but they did not end the open-sea killing of seals. What made pelagic hunting especially destructive was that it consisted of shooting seals from small boats put out from the main vessel. In these rocking, unsteady craft, it was usually impossible to take careful aim or to determine the sex of the animal hunted. Often the shots would wound the seal mortally, and by the time the small boat came around to haul the carcass in, it would have sunk to the bottom. For every seal caught, many others went to the bottom. Then too, most of the seals killed were females in process of bearing young.

As it turned out, the British-American agreement was not successful. This was because depredations on the sealing grounds were carried out not only by English and American sealers, but also by nationals of many other countries. Ships flying foreign flags could venture within three miles of the seal islands and hunt as much as they desired. Now and then, the nearness of the islands tempted the hunters to raid the breeding grounds themselves. Under such circumstances the catch would be great, but its effect on the herd was disastrous. Dwindling of the herd also boosted the value of the skins to new heights.

Mike Healy, the brilliant, impetuous skipper of the *Bear*, knew that he had an almost impossible job on his hands when he arrived on the scene. Nicknamed "Hell Roaring" Mike by the men who served under him, Healy was one of the most colorful men ever to command a famous ship. By the time he assumed command of the *Bear* he had already established a reputation as a fine navigator and a good officer in the northland. As a first lieutenant on the cutter *Rush*, he had patrolled the Pacific coast. His experience in the territory dated from 1868, when as a young officer he had made his first trip north. By 1881 "Cap'n Mike" was a seasoned and experienced skipper in northern waters. By the time he completed his Pacific cruise in 1895 he was being hailed as a legendary figure.

His first reaction to his new command was not particularly enthusiastic. In an official communication to the Secretary of the Treasury, he wrote:

I would respectfully call the serious attention of the Department to the fact that nineteen feet of water, which I understand is the draught of the *Bear*, is altogether too great to make her an effective cruiser on the shore of the Arctic Ocean. With such a draught, all effectiveness as a cruiser against contraband trade and as an aid to vessels that might become stranded would be seriously impaired if not totally destroyed.

Healy was not as good a prophet as he was a sailor. One trip on the *Bear* showed him how much he had underestimated his ship. The ship which Healy thought unfit for Arctic duty served a forty-one-year tour on the Alaskan Patrol, crusing north forty-two times on patrols which averaged approximately 15,000 miles each. Each year the *Bear's* trip north marked the opening of navigation to commercial vessels to Alaskan and Arctic waters. Her return to San Francisco signaled the end of the season.

Under Healy's command, the *Bear* became known to the Eskimos as Healy's *Puk Oomiak* (Healy's Fire Canoe). Later the natives named her the *Nanuk* (White Bear) because of her figurehead.

5

Mike Healy—
The Man and the Legend

Of all the men who captained the *Bear,* none left a deeper imprint on her history than Hell Roaring Mike Healy. During his ten years as her skipper—1886 to 1896—he achieved wide renown.

Healy had an unusual background. He was one of ten children born to Michael Healy, an Irish immigrant to Georgia, and Mary Eliza, a mulatto slave girl who had been a domestic on a neighboring plantation. Healy's eldest brother, James Augustine, became the first Negro Catholic bishop in North America, at Portland, Maine. Another brother, Patrick Francis, served as president of Georgetown University in Washington, D.C. Young Michael did not take to the academic life, and he ran away from school at the age of fifteen to sign on a sailing ship. The sea became his career.

Even before taking command of the *Bear*, Healy had achieved fame as a captain of the revenue cutter *Corwin*. It was probably his success at this duty which led to his new command. To his contemporaries Healy was regarded as an outstanding navigator of northern seas.

In his new assignment he was to have the privilege of commanding the first full-scale patrol of its kind, one which has continued until the present day. His fleet consisted of three cutters, *Rush, Corwin,* and his own vessel, *Bear*. It was an inadequate force for so great a task. Healy's numerous jobs included administration of justice, bringing of medical and other aid to natives, making weather and ice reports, preparation of navigation charts, rescue of vessels in distress, transportation of special passengers and supplies, and fighting seal poachers and other violators of federal laws. In her long tour of Alaskan waters the *Bear* sailed all the way to Point Barrow, the northernmost tip of North America, returning to her home port, San Francisco, usually in October.

The job facing Healy in his new command was enough to dishearten most men. Almost the first order he received was to "seize any vessel found sealing in the Bering Sea." The order was simple; but actually it was a gigantic task, and Healy's means for carrying it out were pitifully inadequate. Against hordes of hardened seal poachers, the United States had sent the three cutters of the first Bering Sea Patrol. In 1886, when Healy took command of the *Bear*, the sealing war had reached its height. Knowledge that the government was making a determined effort to crack down on the practice stimulated many hunters to make one last prodigious effort.

Healy was shrewd enough to know that the only way he could make any headway against the poachers was to make up in sternness and determination what he lacked in facilities. A few tough examples of law enforcement would go a long way toward discouraging the hunters. One of his first crackdowns came in 1887, when the Bering Sea fleet captured twelve Canadian schooners. Gradually a pattern developed. At first the sealers would bluster and protest their innocence. When this failed to get results, they became angry and abusive, threatening to charge the United States with piracy. None of this, however, deterred the tough Mike Healy from doing his duty. Each captured vessel was sent south to Sitka under a prize crew. In spite of loud and irate protests from Great Britain, Healy stuck to his guns.

In that same year, while the *Bear* lay at anchor with the whaling fleet at Port Clarence, a whaler, the *Young Phoenix*, entered the harbor and dropped anchor. Then a small boat was put over the side and made directly for the *Bear*. One of the boat's passengers, the captain of the *Young Phoenix*, hurried up the gangway and showed Healy a piece of wood with enigmatic symbols carved on it:

"J.B.V. Bk. Nap. Tobacco give;
S.W.C. Nav.M. 10 Help come."

The cryptic message had been thrown on board the *Young Phoenix* by an Eskimo who had paddled out to her in his kayak. For a long time the men studied the message. Gradually they began to understand its meaning. They remembered that the bark *Napoleon* had been wrecked on the Siberian coast late in the previous year. Fourteen of her crew of thirty-six had been saved. Others were believed to have made it safely to shore, but they had died later of exposure and starvation.

The symbols in the message referred to J.B. Vincent of Edgartown, Massachusetts, one of the *Napoleon's* boat steerers, who had promised tobacco to the bearer of the message. Vincent was now 10 miles southwest of Cape Navarin and needed help.

Within minutes after decoding the message, the *Bear* was under way. After steaming 400 miles at full speed for two days, she reached the barren shore of Cape Navarin. From the deck *Bear* crewmen could see two ragged men stagger out of a hut on the beach. A boat was sent quickly through the surf. The men were taken on board and looked after. A few days later they were given transportation to San Francisco.

By 1892 the *Bear, Rush,* and *Corwin,* the revenue

Colorful and controversial "Hell Roaring" Mike Healy. The skipper of the *Bear* for many years, he became a legend in Alaskan waters.

cutters which then constituted the Bering Sea Patrol, had made so many seizures of sealers that there was international tension. The British took the position that the seizures were illegal, since they were for the most part outside the three-mile offshore limit, which was recognized as being under the jurisdiction of the United States government. They also argued that seals, as wild animals, were lawful prey to anyone. The United States countered with the argument that the Bering Sea was under its jurisdiction, then went on to stress its determination that the killing of mother seals would not be permitted.

Just when it appeared that matters had reached the breaking point, both countries decided to turn the entire affair over to an international arbitration tribunal. The British agreed not to oppose any seizures while the case was being considered by the court.

The *Bear* was ordered by the government to continue her duties as before. The slaughter of the seals went on with undiminished fury, for the hunters paid no attention to the legal proceedings and made devastating inroads on the herds.

The result of the proceedings in the international court was unfortunate for the United States. The court declared the Bering Sea an open sea and, therefore, available to ships of any nationality. To the men of the *Bear*, as well as to their comrades on the other cutters of the patrol, it seemed as though the labor of the past several years had been futile. Nevertheless, the patrol continued to guard the seal islands and to convoy the seal herds on their annual migration.

The terrible butchery did not come to an end until 1911, when a treaty was signed by the four countries primarily involved; Great Britain, Japan, Russia, and the United States. The treaty prohibited all seal hunt-

The *Bear* was always a great favorite with Alaskan natives. Here Eskimos visit the ship at Kotzebue Sound, Alaska.

ing in the North Pacific and the Bering Sea. Only the natives were permitted to hunt seals for their own use with their primitive equipment. Instead of putting the seal islands under the control of a private company, the United States undertook their guardianship. A system of fur-seal conservation was begun, permitting only a limited number to be killed each year. The senseless massacre of the seal herds was over. The original treaty ended in 1941, but it was renewed in 1957 and once again in 1963.

Today the estimated seal population is about 1,750,000, or about eight and one-half times the total in 1911. Biologists have estimated that the seal herd is growing too large and should be reduced to an optimum number of approximately 1,500,000. The foundation for this great accomplishment in marine resource conservation was laid by Mike Healy and his patrol.

Among Healy's concerns was the steady decrease of the Eskimo population. In the 1890's the term "genocide" had not yet come into use. Yet this was precisely what had been going on in the years since the United States had taken possession of territory. The impact of the white men's culture on the primitive natives had been devastating. Not only had the coming of the white hunters upset the native pattern of life, but it had introduced the Eskimo to the effects of alcohol.

Though the government had taken stern measures to halt the sale of alcoholic beverages to Eskimos, greed overcame all scruples. Nor was alcohol the only factor in the situation. The unrestrained killing of seals, walruses, salmon, and other sea creatures had deprived the natives of their principal source of food and clothing. Virtually their entire economy was built on hunting. Thus, when the white hunters came to

Alaska, they brought the possible destruction of an entire people. The odds against Eskimo survival were further increased by an unwise regulation prohibiting Eskimos from using repeating rifles. This put them at a great disadvantage in the competition for vitally needed game. It was a classic example of what can happen when an advanced, aggressive culture comes into contact with a primitive one.

The suffering and wretchedness of the natives stirred the compassionate side of Healy's nature. He was profoundly impressed by an incident which took place in 1890 during his annual spring visit to King Island.

As the *Bear* approached the island, the men on board could see that the shore was crowded with strangely quiet natives. Craft put out for the *Bear,* and Eskimos climbed aboard her. Starvation made the bones stand out in their faces; they were so weak that they could hardly beg for food. Healy knew they were a proud people, ordinarily scorning charity.

The chief told him that more than 200 of his tribe had died of starvation in the winter. Only 100 men and women were still alive on King Island. The walrus, on which they normally depended for food, had not appeared during the previous fall. Savage winter storms had blocked the passage to the mainland. Those who had managed to stay alive had been reduced to eating dogs and seaweed.

Before heading for Point Barrow, Healy ordered

food supplies ferried ashore. His men also built platforms in accordance with Eskimo custom for the burial of the dead. Gradually the pitiful remainder of the community was nursed back to health. The experience reinforced Healy's resolve to do something about preventing another such tragedy. Another spectator of the incident was a special passenger, Dr. Sheldon Jackson, general agent for education in Alaska since 1885. As the *Bear* moved north, the two men discussed the problem earnestly.

Dr. Jackson was a missionary and an eloquent speaker. He was dedicated to the cause of educating the natives and the establishment of good government for the territory, and his speeches had already produced some significant results in Alaska.

Healy and Jackson realized that unless something could be done quickly there was a possibility the Eskimo race would wipe out. Healy remembered that the Siberian Chukchi looked healthy and well fed in contrast with the Eskimos and that like the Lapps of northern Scandinavia, they were herders of reindeer. Was it a solution to the problem? But several formidable obstacles had to be overcome. Reindeer had to be procured from the Chukchi who had superstitions about selling live animals. And if the reindeer were purchased, they would have to be transported across the Bering Sea to Alaska. Equally formidable was the matter of reorienting the Eskimos from a hunting

(Official U.S. Coast Guard Photograph)

Deer being hoisted aboard the *Bear* at Seniavine Strait, Siberia, in 1891. Domesticated deer were purchased and taken to Alaska to rescue natives from starvation and to start them in deer husbandry.

to a pastoral mode of life. Jackson was enough of a realist to know that persuading Washington of the practicality of the proposal would not be easy. But he was a determined man. He was sure the Eskimos could be taught to adjust to a new way of life.

Congress did not react enthusiastically to Jackson's suggestion. Nevertheless, he succeeded in raising

$2,000 from the general public for the purchase of reindeer. It would be a purely experimental project. But if it worked, it could be expanded to permit larger purchases.

In the summer of 1891 the *Bear*, with Dr. Jackson on board, sailed up and down more than 1,500 miles of the Siberian coast to purchase the first reindeer. At Seniavine Strait, Siberia, twelve reindeer were purchased from Quoharie, a Chukchi deerman, and landed at Unalaska.

During the next decade revenue cutters brought some 1,100 reindeer to Alaska. Dr. Jackson's Bureau of Education took charge of the deer on landing and distributed them among government and mission schools which trained the natives in reindeer culture. Each graduate received the nucleus of a herd from which to breed additional deer.

Although most people were not aware of it at the time, the introduction of reindeer to Alaska represented a significant social experiment. Its objective was nothing less than to change the way of life of an entire people from the primitive culture of the hunter to the more advanced civilization of a pastoral society. Ordinarily such social change comes about slowly and painfully over centuries. In Alaska, however, two men were telescoping a dramatic sociological change into a short span of slightly more than a decade.

By 1940 the domesticated reindeer herds in Alaska had risen to an estimated 500,000, providing both food and clothing for the native population. Healy, who would

One of the crews which sailed on the *Bear*. This photo was taken in 1895.

have been the last to look on himself as a social reformer, had helped accomplish a near miracle. The importation of reindeer into Alaska stands out as one of the most constructive measures ever carried out by the United States in Alaska. It remains a monument to the memory of two dedicated men blessed with the American pioneering spirit.

One of Healy's most unusual law enforcement cases took place in the spring of 1893. Word had been received that H. R. Thornton, a missionary and schoolmaster at Teller, had been murdered by Eskimo boys. According to the report, Thornton, a stern, self-righteous man, had threatened to whip three boys, including the chief's son.

It was the worst possible form of punishment he could have meted out to a proud people who dreaded physical humiliation above all things. The records also indicate that Thornton had never succeeded in establishing any real communication with the people among whom he lived. To him the Eskimos were an inferior breed of humans.

Faced with the intolerable indignity of a whipping, the boys decided that Thornton must be killed. They went to his house, and when he answered their knock, they shot him through the chest.

The noise of the gunshot soon brought other Eskimos to the scene. Shocked by the criminal act, they stoned two of the boys to death, then dug a grave for the chief's son. When the grave was completed, the boy lay down in it and announced that he was thirsty. So the entire village escorted him back to his home, where he had his last drink. He was then led back to his grave, and his personal treasures were laid beside him. His uncle, his nearest kin, pointed a rifle at his head and carried out the grisly judgment of execution.

When Healy heard of the matter, he was puzzled about a course of action. How could you explain Anglo-Saxon concepts of trial procedure to a primitive people with a literal sense of justice? Undoubtedly the boys were deserving of punishment, but whether they had merited so awful a penalty was another question. It was indeed a puzzler, but Healy handled it in his usual adroit fashion.

Pointing out that he could not condone the manner in which judgment had been carried out, he nevertheless recognized and praised the elementary sense of justice which had impelled the Eskimos to take such action. He warned them, however, that in the future such severe punishment could only be dispensed by a court of law. All through the early years of the patrol, skippers of the Revenue Cutter Service had the same problem. They had to instill nineteenth-century values into a people still living in a far earlier age. Amazingly, they succeeded to a large extent.

By 1896, when Healy left the *Bear*, a new wave of migration to Alaska had begun. It had been started by the discovery of gold in Canada's Klondike. Although the Klondike was across the border in Canada, the routes to it lay through Alaska. Within a year or two, other gold strikes in Alaska, near Nome and in the Tanana Valley, transformed the gold rush into a tidal wave of migration.

The revenue cutters were now faced with new and

bigger problems. In addition to the lawlessness of whalers and poachers, they had on their hands a host of new problems. The Eskimo, whose primitive way of life had already been corrupted by the earlier invasion of the white man, was exposed to even greater dangers. The problem of keeping liquor from the natives, difficult enough before, was now almost beyond solution with the relatively few ships and men available to the Revenue Cutter Service in Alaska. Many of the newcomers were highly skilled in bribery and corruption. Theirs was not the simple lawlessness of men who out of sheer boredom sometimes got drunk.

Captain Francis Tuttle, the man who replaced Healy, had his work cut out for him. Tuttle contrasted sharply with his predecessor. He was a relaxed, easygoing sailor, who prided himself on his enormous mustache which was carefully combed and which was a good 10 inches in span. Old-timers also recall that he was something of a dandy and very fond of the ladies. Accompanying him was a thin young lieutenant, Claude S. Cochran, who had become greatly interested in the *Bear* and had requested duty on her. He became the navigator.

The *Bear*'s status as a good, tough ship and the generally high esteem in which the Revenue Cutter Service was held in the north were major assets for Tuttle. They were Healy's legacy to him.

6

The Bear Against the Arctic

There was an important difference between the tasks facing Captain Tuttle and those that had concerned Mike Healy. Healy had been concerned with preserving Alaska's marine resources, primarily its seals, as well as with the protection of the native population. Tuttle also had these responsibilities. But his job was made more difficult by the drifters, spongers, and brawlers whom the gold strikes had brought to Alaska.

To Tuttle and his small fleet it was a relatively simple matter to handle an occasional uprising on a whaler or mistreatment of a native. But these newcomers were of a different stripe. They were often smooth operators who knew how to work just within the law. It was clear that Alaska Territory was entering a new phase and that the mushrooming of cities and new communities was creating a host of problems.

At the same time whalers were still getting into trouble and requiring aid. In the fall of 1897 the *Bear* was at Seattle, en route south to San Francisco after her seasonal tour in northern waters. Returning whalers brought word that eight whaling vessels, with crews totaling some 265 men, were helplessly caught in the ice pack off Point Barrow, Alaska. The annual breakup of ice would not occur for at least eight or nine months.

Men who knew the bitter Arctic winter shuddered at the possible fate of the men. Some of the whalers were sure to be crushed before the winter was over. Although it was possible for the whalemen to make their way across the ice to other ships or to Point Barrow, none had sufficient provisions for the trek. Barrow itself had limited supplies. The nearest supplies were hundreds of miles away, and winter travel through the frozen north was impossible. Thus 265 men faced death by starvation.

The owners of the whalers and San Francisco authorities appealed to President William McKinley for help. He, in turn, referred the matter to the Treasury Department. Secretary of the Treasury Lyman Gage inquired about the feasibility of undertaking a rescue mission. But the earliest that a ship could get through the ice would be July or August, by which time the whalers would probably be dead. The only hope was to send a cutter as far north as she could go and then to put an expedition ashore to make the rest of the perilous journey to the whalers. It was at best a forlorn hope. However, an effort had to be made. Recognizing the peril of the journey, Secretary Gage sent a detailed letter of instructions to Captain Tuttle, with a carefully laid-out course of action.

Captain Tuttle went into action immediately after receiving the Secretary's instructions. In answer to a call for volunteers, since this was outside normal service duties, every member of his officers and crew responded. To head the overland relief party, he chose Lieutenant David H. Jarvis, a veteran of eight years of Alaskan service. This slight-looking man possessed extraordinary hardihood. Under Jarvis would be Second Lieutenant Ellsworth P. Bertholf, later captain commandant of the Coast Guard, and Dr. Samuel J. Call, a ship's surgeon. To this group, the authorities in Washington added F. Koltchoff, an experienced reindeer man. Inclusion of Koltchoff in the expedition was necessitated by the bold plan to collect a herd of reindeer on the overland trek. They would serve the double purpose of transportation and food for the whaling men on arrival at Point Barrow. It was a daring plan, and there was an outside chance that it would succeed. But the odds were heavily against it. A 1,500-mile trek over the frozen wastes of Alaska in the teeth of an Arctic winter was an undertaking that had never been attempted before.

As the *Bear* moved north, Tuttle and Jarvis carefully worked out their plans. The reindeer which Healy and

Jackson had imported into Alaska only a few years before were at the heart of the plan. The original small herd had grown into three herds. There was one at the Teller Reindeer Station, a second at Cape Prince of Wales, belonging to the American Missionary Society, and a third belonging to Charlie Artisarlook, an Eskimo, at Point Rodney. Jarvis was supposed to take over the latter two herds, assuming that their owners could be persuaded to part with them.

Tuttle had not been under way long before he discovered that the ice pack was a good deal farther south than he had anticipated. Reconnaissance of the southern edge of the ice failed to reveal any open water. He was face to face with the bad news that the *Bear* would not be able to reach the shore north of Cape Vancouver. This meant that the overland expedition would have to travel twice as far as the original plans had contemplated.

Impatiently Tuttle waited for an opening in the ice so that he could effect a landing on the cape. It finally happened on a dreary December 16, when the pack drifted seaward, permitting the *Bear* to anchor off the cape.

In that desolate setting, under constant assault of icy seas, the whaleboat crews ferried Jarvis and their supplies ashore. But their luck did not hold out. On the return trip for a second load, the ice started to close in. Heavy fragments of ice smashed into the *Bear*. The vessel was now in a very precarious position, caught between the pack and the shore. Tuttle chose to drive into the ice floes, pushing them aside, desperately seeking sea room.

Quickly the boats made a second trip to the beach, carrying dogs and more supplies. After they were hoisted in, the *Bear* moved into an open lead, heading west.

The *Bear* managed to slam her way through the ice pack, completing the passage to Unalaska. The men of the *Bear* were amazed to see how gold fever had changed this normally quiet place into a roaring waiting point for prospectors. More than 1,000 men had settled in or near the town, waiting to sail north to the Yukon in the spring. All that Tuttle could do at this point was to wait for spring. Meanwhile, his knowledge of the whereabouts and progress of the expedition would be limited to such scraps of information as could be furnished from time to time by whalemen.

In choosing Jarvis to head the expedition, Captain Tuttle had made an excellent decision. Jarvis was a resourceful, hardy man capable of meeting emergencies without panicking. The small boats which had put him ashore after leaving the *Bear* landed near Tununak, close to Cape Vancouver. The beach there was at the base of a range of mountains and strewn with heavy rocks and boulders. Realizing that the terrain was too rugged for traveling by dog sled, Jarvis engaged a half-breed trader, Alexis Kalenin, to transport the outfit to the village by water. After reaching the village, Jarvis immediately set about acquiring the means for travel. Fortunately for Jarvis, the village of Tununak had a good supply of Alas-

Captain Francis Tuttle, skipper of the *Bear*, at the time of the epic overland expedition for the relief of the crews of the whaling vessels stranded in the Arctic Ocean.

kan huskies. In addition to providing the dogs, Alexis offered to serve as a guide across the Yukon Delta country. Several other natives were also to come along in the same capacity. According to Alexis' reckoning, St. Michael could be reached in about twelve days if the weather remained favorable and the sleds were not too heavily loaded. That would be the first objective. But it was only a fraction of the 1,500-mile trek which must be made with all possible haste.

Jarvis was anxious to get started at once on the journey, but Kalenin pointed out that the dogs were still exhausted from a previous journey and would require at least one day's rest. It was decided, therefore, to postpone the trek until the morning of December 18.

There was a surprise in store for Jarvis. The *Bear*, which he thought had departed on December 16, could be seen on the horizon on the seventeenth. Kalenin and Koltchoff went down to investigate and returned with supplies and dogs which had not come ashore the previous day. These included two sleds, seven dogs, and some dried fish for food.

From Kalenin, Jarvis also learned that native villages were scattered at convenient distances along the route to the Yukon and that a settlement could be reached each night. This made it unnecessary to carry large quantities of dog food which could slow travel. Jarvis also had an opportunity to notice that the sleds made in Seattle were heavy and cumbersome, compared to native sleds, which were light and strong and thoroughly adapted to the needs of the country. Therefore, he decided to take three native sleds and one from the ship. Now he was ready for the perilous voyage.

On the morning of December 18 the expedition set out on the first leg of the journey to Ukogamute, on the northern shore of Nelson Island. Jarvis and his group reached Ukogamute on schedule after great hardship. But this was only a small foretaste of many other difficulties to be encountered during the approximately 200-mile journey to St. Michael. In the thirteen days that it took them to reach St. Michael, they had to pass over rocky beaches, rough shore ice, endure raging storms and deep snow, and cross mountain ranges in temperatures many degrees below zero. At the end of each day the men's exhaustion was so great that it didn't seem possible they could go on the following morning. But somehow, out of some unknown reserve of strength, the party kept on. The Eskimos regarded the project as senseless and foolhardy. When they were only one day's journey from St. Michael, Jarvis and Call lost the track in a blinding snowstorm. Exhausted, half-frozen, and bruised from stumbling in the darkness, they found sanctuary in a native village.

Jarvis' first move on reaching St. Michael was to contact Lieutenant Colonel George M. Randall, commander of the military post. There he learned that the reindeer herd at the Teller Station was unavailable because it was to be used in relieving a group of gold prospectors stranded on the Upper Yukon. In his emphatic way, Jarvis made it clear that if the whalemen were to be saved, reindeer from the herds at Cape Prince of Wales and Point Rodney would have to reach them not later than April, when food supplies would be exhausted. But an enormous journey lay ahead of the expedition. They were 500 miles away from Point Clarence, the next important destination. And after making that difficult trek, there remained another 800 miles to Point Barrow--all of this at the worst time of the year. To reach Barrow within the scheduled time would demand the utmost exertion on the part of men and dogs. Randall understood

Jarvis' predicament and gave an order for Dr. A. N. Kettleson, superintendent of the reindeer herd at Teller Station, to give assistance in speeding Jarvis along on his journey.

Jarvis was especially concerned about the dogs, which had already traveled 375 miles and were completely exhausted. So great was his haste to push on that he did not wait for the dogs to recuperate but secured new teams. He also refitted the members of his group with deerskin clothing which was lighter and warmer than the dogskin and woolen clothing they had brought from the ship.

Some two days after leaving St. Michael, the expedition met Mr. Tilton, third mate of the steam whaler *Belvedere*. He had left Point Barrow on October 17, and his ship had been frozen in at the Sea Horse Islands on the twenty-first. The long, hard journey had left him and his dog team exhausted.

Tilton told Jarvis that the whalers *Orca, Jesse H. Freeman,* and *Belvedere* had got past Point Barrow and down the coast as far as the Sea Horse Islands before becoming imprisoned by the ice. At this point the *Orca* had been crushed, and the *Freeman* had been trapped and abandoned. Both crews had gone on board the *Belvedere*, which had managed to move around Point Franklin, where it put into winter quarters. Jarvis also learned that the *Rosario* was close to Point Barrow on the west side and that the *Newport, Fearless,* and *Jeanie* were strung along the shore at various distances east of Point Barrow.

The whaling ship *Wanderer* had last been seen 60 miles west of Herschel Island, early in September. The wreck of the *Navarch* was drifting about in the ice east of Point Barrow.

This was discouraging news for Jarvis. The loss of the *Orca* and the *Freeman* with their provisions made his position much worse than he had anticipated. The men trapped in the ice now had even less to sustain them than before, with a grim winter ahead.

On January 5 Jarvis set out from Unalaklik with three light sleds. He had to break his promise to return his dog teams to their owners since he had been unable to obtain replacements. However, he was able to secure a better tent and stove, deerskin sleeping bags, deerskin socks, boots, and mittens, along with cloth shoes for the dogs. This was no small item since the dogs wore out a set of shoes on each day's trek. At last Jarvis considered himself ready for the next big push.

The weather, unusually warm for that time, made the going even harder. The men had to contend with soft snow and steep climbs up mountainsides. By January 8 the snow had become so heavy that the men had to wear snowshoes. Sometimes the dogs would sink out of sight in the steep drifts. It became necessary for four of the men to walk ahead of the team to trample down a path. The huskies, justly renowned for their tremendous endurance and strength, could only travel about 10 miles a day before succumbing to exhaustion.

But the northland had not used all its weapons against

the hard-pressed group. It grew colder, and for days on end the thermometer never rose above zero. Relentlessly Jarvis drove the expedition onward until, on January 11, it reached Golovin Bay, where he dismissed the dog teams and sent them back to St. Michael.

At Golovin Bay Jarvis hired four special Lapland freight sleds. They looked like boats and were pulled by reindeer. He also engaged a tough Laplander, Mikkel, along with deerherders, to manage the animals. The group was then joined by Dr. Kettleson. But driving reindeer was a very different matter from handling dogs. Compared to the savage huskies, the reindeer were sensitive and easily frightened. They greatly feared the vicious dogs and at night had to be sheltered from alarming sounds.

Gales and blinding snowstorms slowed the expedition's advance to a crawl. One night Jarvis, who handled the rear sled, was lost in the darkness when his deer ran the sled against a stump, broke his harness and ran away. Wisely, Jarvis crawled into his sleeping bag, hoping his absence would be discovered before he froze to death. His reindeer caught up with the rest of the party and trotted behind the others in the darkness. Jarvis' absence was finally noticed when the team handlers stopped to consult with a chief. They turned back and found Jarvis about an hour later.

With Kettleson and two natives, Jarvis pushed on west, fighting blizzards and storms all the way. After days of hardship, they reached the house of Charlie

Artisarlook at Point Rodney, not far from Cape Nome.

There Jarvis had a difficult task. He was aware that reindeer represented the Eskimo's most important asset —his food, clothing, wealth. It took a long time to build a herd, and its loss was disastrous. Jarvis gave his word that Artisarlook's herd would be replaced, noting also that the *Bear* had been responsible for the introduction of reindeer into Alaska. Only Artisarlook and his herd could complete the long, arduous journey with the deer. The welfare of the remaining women and children could be looked after by neighboring natives. What made Jarvis' job more difficult was that he and Charlie were old friends. He was putting their friendship to the severest test possible. If anything went wrong, Charlie would be abandoning his wife and children to possible starvation.

Charlie and his wife talked it over earnestly. Finally, to Jarvis' immense relief, the decision was favorable. Charlie said that he and his wife were sorry for the white men at Point Barrow and would be glad to help. They would let Jarvis have the deer, their most precious possession in the world, on the strength of Jarvis' promise to replace them.

Jarvis issued food for the natives, collected the deer, and made ready for the 800-mile journey into the Arctic. Since he had to collect more deer at Port Clarence, he left Dr. Call behind to organize the transport of Artisarlook's 133 reindeer. Then he pressed on with Mikkel and Kettleson for the Teller Reindeer Station near Port Clarence. Soon a new difficulty arose. When the deer began to tire, Jarvis sought to hire dog teams—and ran into trouble. Although the Eskimos told Jarvis they did not have sufficient dogs for his purpose, their real objection was that they had no stomach for setting out in a furious storm at 40° below. Jarvis' plans suffered a further blow when Kettleson and Mikkel decided to turn back since they had agreed to accompany him only as far as Artisarlook's village. Only two Eskimos would go along with him.

The crucial stage of the journey had now been reached. Jarvis concluded that to survive, he would "do as the people who lived in the country did—to dress, travel, and live as they did, and, if necessary, to eat the same food." The only way to get along was to conform as nearly as possible to the customs of those who already had solved many of the problems of existence in the Arctic climate. It was a good deal more easily said than done. Between the white and Eskimo civilizations lay a chasm of centuries.

Early on the morning of January 23, with the thermometer at 30° below, Jarvis set out for Cape Prince of Wales. At four o'clock Artisarlook suggested they camp for the night, but Jarvis was not yet tired and wanted to go on. Slowly they kept going until darkness set in and they were near Cape York. Now it was Jarvis who was spent and wanted to rest. But Artisarlook pointed out that it was dangerous to camp without wood and that the ice they were on could break through at any minute. They had to get beyond the line of bluffs before stopping. In the darkness, Jarvis stepped through a crack, and his leg was immediately encased in ice to the knee.

Pushing and lifting the sled, the exhausted men and animals dragged along until midnight when they came to an Eskimo hut. Said Jarvis in his journal: "Though it turned out to be horrible, no palace could have been more welcome."

Pushing on the next morning, Jarvis made for another village about 40 miles away. When the party reached it, the men stopped and refreshed themselves with a good meal. There Jarvis also hired a small sled to lighten the load on the one he had.

But if the journey had been rough before, what Jarvis faced now was much worse. All the crushings of the straits between Alaska and Siberia were shoved up against the mountains which sheered abruptly to the sea. Darkness set in long before they had come to the worst of it, and a faint moon gave too little light. Both men and dogs were exhausted and suffering. Once, in helping the sled over a particularly bad place, Jarvis was thrown several feet down a slide, landing on the back of his head with the sled on top of him. His survival was a miracle. Though the mercury was 30° below, he was wet with sweat from the rigors of his work. The sleds were cracked and broken, the dogs played out. Had the ordeal lasted much longer, they could not have made it. But at last they reached the Cape Prince of Wales and the house of Mr. W. T. Lopp, former superintendent of the Teller Reindeer Station and now representing the American Missionary Society.

The arrival of the haggard, exhausted men at the cape in the middle of an Arctic winter naturally took the Lopps entirely by surprise. Such a thing had never happened before. Staring at the frail-looking Jarvis, Lopp wondered how so slight a man could have made so perilous a journey.

After Jarvis told his reasons for making the journey, Lopp was sympathetic. Lopp held the key to the success or failure of the mission. He was an idealistic man, with a sense of responsibility. As the former superintendent of the government-owned Teller Reindeer Station at Port Clarence, he had become one of the foremost experts on reindeer culture. He had learned how to work with the animals, how to use them to maximum advantage, and also how to train Eskimos in their handling. In all these tasks his work as a teacher and missionary was used to the best advantage. If Lopp were willing to volunteer both his services and his herd for the final phase of the expedition, success might be within the expedition's grasp. As the official government representative in this part of the territory and as a missionary, Lopp had a definite obligation to consider the welfare of the native population. Was it right for him to endanger the existence of the natives by giving up the precious herd to the expedition? Also, the decision was not his alone to make. Part of the herd belonged to Lopp personally, part to the American Missionary Association, and a good number were the property of the Eskimos.

Jarvis shrewdly left the matter in Lopp's hands. This was not a man to be bullied. He would do what he felt to be morally right. But as conscientious as Lopp was, he still had human frailties. Jarvis was asking him not only to provide the herd, but also to leave his wife and undertake the cruel journey to Point Barrow. Finally, to Jarvis' great relief, Lopp agreed to help him.

Jarvis made careful preparations for the remainder of the voyage to Point Barrow. Sleds had to be built; the herders had to be fitted with proper clothing; bags, tents, stoves, camp gear, and spare harness and lassos had to be provided. There were still 700 miles to go over the frozen wastes of northern Alaska. And the important thing was to prepare the party to be independent of villages for the entire journey.

Lopp engaged seven herders. A native named Netaxite was left behind to look after Mrs. Lopp.

The reindeer herd gathered by Lopp was joined by additional deer driven from Point Rodney by Artisarlook and Dr. Call. When the expedition started out for Point Barrow on February 3, 1898, it included 438 reindeer and eighteen sleds. Lopp and three herders with light sleds and well-broken deer went behind the herd, keeping it moving smartly. An Eskimo, Tautuk, brought with him a small Lapp dog trained in this work. He continually circled the outer edges of the herd and kept the deer from straying. The dog turned out to be one of the most valuable members of the party.

On the first day the party traveled about 12 miles. But on February 5 the progress had slowed to 8 miles —far too slow a pace to keep to the schedule Jarvis had set for the expedition. After talking it over with Lopp, Jarvis made the decision to leave the herd in his sole charge since he was experienced enough to handle the matter without assistance. Jarvis and Dr. Call would go down to a village on the coast and secure dog teams. Afterward they would go on to Kotzebue Sound, apprise the native population of the coming of the reindeer, and make such arrangements as were necessary to help Lopp. By leaving the party, Jarvis estimated he would relieve Lopp of loads of six sleds. The essential thing was to get the reindeer to Point Barrow. The Eskimos beyond Cape Prince of Wales had never seen domesticated reindeer and might mistake them for wild deer and try to kill them. By traveling ahead of the expedition, Jarvis could forestall this. So he left Lopp, telling him they would meet again in the vicinity of Kotzebue Sound.

Fortune did not favor Jarvis for long. He found that

the Eskimos along that section of the Alaskan coast were very poor and widely scattered. The seal hunting had been bad, and in some places even the dogs had starved. No one had more than two or three dogs, and it looked as though Jarvis would not be able to assemble a dog team. Furthermore, none of the Eskimos would travel farther than a day from home. Consequently the best that Jarvis could do was about 20 to 25 miles a day.

Even when he succeeded in buying or hiring dogs, the animals did not long remain with him. They would chew off the harnesses or ropes and return to their masters. Only chains could hold them securely, and these were almost impossible to obtain. Finally, by bribing, threatening, and offering shiploads of provisions, Jarvis reached the village of Toatut at Cape Espenberg. There more bad luck overtook him. The native guides, hungry for the white man's food, had eaten most of their provisions until all that was left was "a few broken crackers, enough beans for a day and some tea." No one had dared object since the guides were needed for the journey. Once the guides arrived at Toatut, all except one named Perninyuk left the expedition and took their sleds with them. The Eskimos apparently had no faith in Jarvis' story of sledloads of provisions awaiting them at Cape Blossom.

A drearier prospect could scarcely be imagined. Cape Blossom was more than 40 miles away, and none of the natives at Noatut could be induced to make the journey over the ice. Jarvis realized that Lieutenant Bertholf was waiting for him with provisions and wondering what had happened. It had been about two months since the two had separated, and the original traveling schedule had been drastically altered by the bitter weather and the rugged terrain. Jarvis was now about a week behind schedule. There was also the possibility that Bertholf's part in the mission had not been carried out as originally planned. According to the plan, Bertholf and Koltchoff were to journey to the head of Norton Sound and then head across the mountains to the head of Kotzebue Sound. This would eliminate the need for the long and arduous journey around the peninsula where Jarvis had collected the reindeer. In this cold and desolate part of the world, any number of things could have happened to frustrate the plan. If Bertholf failed to make the prearranged rendezvous with the provisions, the whole carefully prepared expedition could fail when success was within its grasp.

Jarvis was frantic to get started once again, but the stubborn natives would not cross the sound.

Then, on the evening of February 11, an Eskimo who had gone out to test the ice returned with the welcome news that it was hard and that they would be able to start the following morning.

On the morning of February 12 Jarvis resumed his trek northward.

At nightfall the Eskimos wanted to pitch camp, but Jarvis would not let them. Now that Bertholf was only a few miles away, he was determined to push on until he linked up with his shipmate. Rations had been reduced to a few crumbs of crackers and some frozen deer meat. No matter what happened, the party was going forward until it met Bertholf.

Jarvis drove the men on until about ten thirty that night, when they reached the village of Kikiktaruk and the house of the Reverend Robert Samms, a Quaker missionary, who with his wife and Miss Hunniccutt, a teacher, had established themselves there the previous summer. Never had Jarvis beheld a more welcome sight.

What made Jarvis happy was that at Kikiktaruk he was able to join forces with Bertholf, as planned. Bertholf had arrived the night before after a grueling journey. Engelstadt, the trader at Unalaklik, who had undertaken to supply Bertholf with dog teams, had failed to carry out his part of the bargain. This had left Bertholf at the mercy of unscrupulous Eskimos. As a result, he had been forced to return to Golovin Bay to obtain seven deer and sleds, with a Lapp and an Eskimo driver to assist him. But he had made it with the precious provisions intact.

The entire day of February 13 was spent in preparing for the final push to Point Barrow. Jarvis decided to keep to the coast, instead of traveling inland. There was one disquieting fact: Lopp and his reindeer had not arrived on schedule. Leaving Bertholf behind to wait for Lopp and the deer herd, Jarvis and Dr. Call prepared to move on to Point Hope. The men struck out on the bitter morning of February 16, with the thermometer registering 35° below zero. Point Hope was about a week's journey, and here Jarvis hoped to receive news of the whalers.

The trip to Point Hope turned out to be almost a triumphal procession. Everywhere the natives extended the utmost cordiality and hospitality to the brave travelers. Even the weather put on a special display of the aurora borealis, or northern lights, for them. Jarvis described them as stretching "in long shooting streamers that gradually worked over the heavens to the opposite horizon, waving back and forth, so close to the earth as to be seemingly within reach."

On February 20 the party pulled up at the house of Mr. Nelson, manager of Liebes and Company's trading and whaling station at Point Hope. There Jarvis received the news he had been waiting for. Ned Arey, from Point Barrow, who had come down to see the men who had ventured so far north in the dead of a northern winter. The news he brought was serious, but not as bad as Jarvis had anticipated. Provisions at Point Barrow were short, but there was enough flour, bread, tea, and coffee to keep the whalers alive until May. The whaling party had been kept together, but there had been three deaths. Scurvy had already made its appearance on the *Belvedere*. Luckily, large numbers of wild deer had come into the surrounding country, and native hunters had sent in enough fresh meat to keep the men from starving.

Nevertheless, the situation was serious. It would be August before the *Bear* could make it to Point Barrow. By that time everyone in the whaling fleet might be dead of starvation.

The important thing now, Jarvis realized, was to send word to the whaling fleet that they had not been forgotten, that help was on the way. At Point Hope Jarvis learned of Lopp's successful but very difficult crossing of Kotzebue Sound. Now he and his herd were traveling up the coast. Jarvis went down the coast and met him at the Kivalina River on February 26. There they decided that Lopp would take his herd by an inland route up the Kivalina River, then cross the mountains to the headwaters of the Pitmegea River on the north side. This route would be safer for both deer and men.

Jarvis struggled back to Point Hope, arriving once more at Nelson's house. The journey had cost him eight days of hard travel. Before him loomed the most difficult phase of the journey. From Point Hope to Point Belcher stretched 300 miles of Arctic waste. He and his men would have to depend on whatever they could carry in the way of food and supplies. Learning there were ample stores at Point Hope to be spared for 100 men, Jarvis contemplated sending some of the icebound whalers there.

It was a hard decision to make. If food supplies at Point Barrow ran out in May, as he had been informed by Arey, it would make little sense to keep 300 men there while there were ample provisions at Point Hope. Jarvis finally decided to send 100 men down from Point Barrow to Point Hope, where he would leave Lieutenant Bertholf to look after the men after they arrived. It was no easy undertaking. The weakened whalers would have to travel a distance of 400 miles, much of it on foot. Provisions would have to be carried or dragged on sleds the entire distance. To simplify the problem, Jarvis instructed Bertholf to transport and place about 500 pounds of flour, tea, bread, and other supplies at the mouth of the Pitmegea River, nearly 100 miles up the coast. The whalers would be started in parties of 10, with a leader, and provisions enough to last to the Pitmegea River.

When Jarvis' party set out on March 6, they had to cut a path through heavy drifts. At Cape Lisburne the weather was especially bitter, and the wind made the going almost impossible. But soon they began to make better progress. At last they arrived at the mouth of the Pitmegea River for a rendezvous with Lopp. Searching for a sign of the deer herd, Jarvis found a cross made of two pieces of a breadbox. In the letter stuck between the boards, Jarvis found Lopp's note, left according to agreement. Lopp had arrived at this point on March 7, three days before. It had taken him six days to cross the mountains, and the sled deer were almost played out; but the herd was in good condition. After one day's rest he had gone ahead.

Now that he was in the final phase of the expedition, Jarvis suddenly found new difficulties. He had loaded all the outfits and dog food on two sleds, sending the extra sled back to Point Hope. But he had not reckoned on the effect that the arrangement would have on the huskies. The tired animals could barely drag the heavily loaded sleds. About all that he could travel on March 11 was eight miles.

As day followed freezing day, Jarvis gave up his dream of catching up with the deer herd. A fierce blizzard stalled the group on March 15. During that same terrible blizzard, Lopp had been compelled to move his camp. (Afterward, when Jarvis had caught up with Lopp many days later, the masses of black skin on their faces and noses showed the ordeal they had undergone.)

On March 21 Jarvis reached an old abandoned house just north of Blossom Shoals, where he and Lopp had planned to meet and make final arrangements for the last part of the journey. Lopp arrived two days later. The men divided their stores of bread and tea, then separated once more until they should meet at Point Barrow.

The party was now less than 100 miles from the imprisoned whaling fleet. Upon reaching the village of Sedaro, Jarvis met John Grubin, employed by the whaling station at Point Barrow. Grubin said that the whalers were in relatively good condition as the result of spring hunting and a supply of fresh meat. But matters were gradually growing worse, and the general level of health was not good. The vessels were in no danger at the present time. Jarvis sent Grubin south with his sled to find Lopp and help him if necessary. He himself drove on to the whaling fleet.

Excitement surged through him as he realized that within a matter of hours his quest would be accomplished. The long nightmare of Arctic cold and suffering had not been in vain. He had accomplished an incredible feat with the odds at least 1,000 to 1 against him. And then it happened. Toward noon, as he crossed the lagoon back of the Sea Horse Islands, he beheld a welcome sight. It was the whaler *Belvedere,* the first of the vessels he had been sent to aid. Housed in and banked up outside with snow, the vessel was almost covered except for her spars and rigging.

On the afternoon of March 25, 1898, the exhausted Jarvis and his gallant band drew alongside the whaler. Going on board, they announced themselves. So great was the shock of their arrival that it was some time before the whalers' astonishment wore off and they could welcome the relief party.

But there was no time for self-congratulation. Jarvis saw at once that Captain Millard was critically sick and possibly would not survive the winter. Thirty men were on board the *Belvedere,* fifteen of her crew having been sent to Point Barrow. Rations were so short that the men had only two small meals a day. Among those aboard were survivors of the crushed whaler *Orca* and the lost *Freeman*.

Seeing that the situation on the *Belvedere* was good, Jarvis decided not to stop but to continue his trek northward to Point Barrow. The following day his party journeyed about 35 miles before stopping for the night. After the long nightmare of the past months, Jarvis could allow himself the luxury of looking back "with a measure of satisfaction." He had good cause for satisfaction. He was on the verge of accomplishing one of the greatest Arctic feats in history. In the heart of an Arctic winter, when even Eskimos would not move more than a scant few miles from their villages, this hardy man and his equally tenacious companions had made a fantastic trip of more than 1,500 miles. They had lived off the country and had also managed the incredible feat of bringing a large herd of nervous reindeer over rough, treacherous ice, endless tundras, and mountains glazed with ice.

The weather relented on March 29, when the expedition reached Point Barrow on a clear, beautiful morning. Passing rapidly through the village, Jarvis made directly for Cape Smythe, about nine miles south of Point Barrow, where the whalemen were camped. What happened after the gallant rescuers arrived is best described by Jarvis.

> All the population came out to see us go by and wondered what strange outfit it was, and when we greeted Mr. Brower [manager of the Smythe Whaling and Trading Company], and some of the

officers of the wrecked vessels, whom we knew, they were stunned, and it was some time before they could realize that we were flesh and blood. Some looked off to the south to see if there was not a ship in sight, and others wanted to know if we had come up in a balloon. Though they had realized their dangerous situation last fall and had sent out Mr. Tilton and Mr. Walker for aid with the first opening of the ice, they had not thought it possible for anyone to reach them in winter, and had not we and our positions been so well known, I think they would have doubted that we really did come in from the outside world.

But while the epic overland trek was done, Jarvis' work was not over. The man who had taken the worst that an Arctic winter could hurl at him was now confronted by other problems. He was appalled to see the filthy, verminous place in which the men were quartered. The roof was open in places but had been patched up. One window gave a feeble light to a single large room occupied by about eighty men. To keep warm, some of the men had boxed in their berths. In these boxes they kept improvised seal-oil lamps burning. Soot and smoke covered everything, including the men's clothing and faces. Some had been so weakened and demoralized by their ordeal that they could barely walk. Only the cold had prevented an epidemic of sickness.

Dr. Call reported four cases of scurvy, and all the men were affected to some degree. Although the rescue party had no antiscorbutics, the fresh meat they had brought with them would help to prevent a spread of scurvy.

Coolly and methodically, Jarvis went about his new job of caring for the whalemen. Meanwhile, Lopp who had completed his part of the expedition, left his herd, and started back for his home. He used the dog team which Jarvis and Call had driven north.

Jarvis increased the fresh-meat ration of the whalers to two and one-half pounds a week. The filthy bedding was taken out and aired. All the heavy deerskins that could be brought in by the hunters were distributed to the neediest of the whalemen. Once the Eskimos found out what was wanted, they started to supply clothing which they had put away for future use. Long weeks of living in filth had made it habitual to some of the whalers. It was difficult to induce them to cleanse themselves with the soap that Jarvis provided. But gradually the dirty, bedraggled group of men began to shape up into a more self-respecting, orderly unit.

While the whalers were recovering from their experience, Jarvis saw to it that they kept away from the local people. The Eskimos were also told not to permit any of the white men to live with them. The Eskimo supply of food was already scarce owing to the generous contributions which had been made during the winter months to the stranded whalers. In some cases, this had led to semistarvation among the good-hearted Eskimos.

It was time for Jarvis to turn his attention to the other members of the whaling fleet. Within the next several

Officers of the overland expedition. *Left:* Second Lieutenant E. P. Bertholf. *Center:* Surgeon S. J. Call. *Right:* First Lieutenant J. H. Jarvis, Commanding.

weeks he worked at an incredible pace to offset some of the damage done by the awful cold of a north Alaskan winter. Both during the push north and during the relief operations at the site of the locked-in whaling ships, Jarvis had proved himself an inspiring, resolute leader of men. He was in every sense of the word a hero. Not only had he performed a near miracle in saving the whalemen, but he had achieved the greatest victory of all, triumph over his own very human doubts and weaknesses.

The ice had begun to open in the Bering Strait, and the *Bear* was now ready to start the voyage north. Her progress was slow, but she pushed steadily through the ice pack. A few miles west of Point Barrow, a party from the lost whaler *Orca*, heading south in accordance with Jarvis' instructions, sighted the *Bear* and boarded her. Captain Sherman, skipper of the *Orca*, brought the welcome news that, thanks to the work of Jarvis and Dr. Call, the men at Point Barrow were in good condition. Sherman was also pleased to see Lieutenant Bertholf, who had come on board the *Bear* at Point Hope.

When the *Bear* finally reached Barrow on July 28, 1898, it was a gala occasion. Tuttle gave a hero's greeting to Jarvis and his crew. In the log for that day, however, was the laconic entry: "Lieut. Jarvis reported on board. Duty with Overland Expedition completed."

So famous had the *Bear* become that the words "I'm from the *Bear*" automatically assured a seaman of a royal welcome anywhere along the coast. A grateful nation showed its pride in the expedition by awarding gold medals to Jarvis, Bertholf, and Call. After her hard service in the north, the *Bear* was ordered to Mare Island for general overhaul.

7

The Old Order Changes

The *Bear* continued her legendary ways. In the summer of 1899 she preceded an armada of privately owned vessels bearing gold hunters toward the Yukon. News had come through that a new rich strike had been discovered on Anvil Creek near Cape Nome. When the prospectors in the area heard of it, they immediately shifted operations to that site.

All through the winter few outside prospectors had heard of this development. But with the coming of spring, Nome City turned into a huge mining camp. Although there were scarcely any accommodations, new shiploads of prospectors arrived to add their confusion to the existing chaos.

The *Bear* became a frequent visitor to the gold-crazy city of Nome. The summer of 1900 witnessed a huge wave of migration which made the preceding ones look unimportant. The Klondike had been largely worked out, and the big prizes were gone. Nome became the new Eldorado which all the prospectors sought. The Yukon River was thronged by boats of every description, bringing in new hordes of gold seekers. A real bonanza was reaped by owners of ships on the San Francisco-Alaska run. The once placid Yukon River was now crowded with ships of all kinds. Almost anything that floated could be found there. Thirty-two thriving companies were operating on it, and their fleet included 600 steamers, 8 tugs, and 20 barges. So anxious were the gold seekers to reach the Klondike that they were willing to pay outrageous prices for crowded, dirty, uncomfortable transportation to the mining area.

By the time the *Bear* returned to Nome the following summer the migration to Alaska was in full swing. The flood of gold-hungry prospectors swarming into Nome made the past year's migration seem almost unimportant. The primeval solitude which had once gripped the endless tundra of the Seward Peninsula was forever shattered by the new hard-drinking, brawling city of Nome, numbering more than 15,000.

The vessel represented what little humanity there was in the cruel, hard world of the gold rush. At one time several prospectors, while visiting in Nome to rest and buy supplies, reported to Captain Tuttle that a number of Eskimo villages were being devastated by influenza

A few of the crewmen from trapped whaling vessels rescued by the *Bear's* overland expedition to Point Barrow, Alaska.

and measles. Responsive as always, the *Bear* prepared to undertake a mercy mission.

First, the Bear sailed to the Teller Reindeer Station, where she took a number of deer on board. Then she visited the native villages. At some of the settlements visitors from the *Bear* found that many Eskimos had died of disease and the survivors had been so weakened as to be unable to hunt for food. The story was substantially the same on King Island, Big and Little Diomede, Point Hope, and Point Barrow.

Medicine and food were landed and deer distributed.

The sick were cared for and the dead given proper burial. Actions such as this did more to persuade the local people of the goodwill of the American government than many more ambitious undertakings.

The work of the *Bear* and its sister ships on patrol was made harder by dishonest shipping agents who often assured prospectors of the great wealth in the bleak Kotzebue area. All kinds of ridiculous stories were deliberately circulated about miraculous strikes, and men, always ready to believe in the possibility of vast, sudden wealth, headed toward it by the thousands. What they found was not wealth, but hardship, disease and suffering. More often than not they turned to the *Bear* for help on the return trip south.

Through the years the *Bear* labored in northern seas. In 1907 the hardy ship was thirty-four years old. She had more than lived up to her promise, but it had become evident that changes would have to be made to bring her into the modern era. At the Mare Island Navy Yard, her worn Scots boiler was removed and a modern water-tube type installed. The water-rotted yellow pine which had sheathed her hull for so many years was ripped away and replaced with tough Douglas fir. New quarters were built on the deck for her warrant officers. Electric lights replaced the oil lamps. Workmen at Mare Island installed a distiller to ease the probem of watering the ship, and the *Bear* received her first low-power radio with a range of nearly 100 miles. This was installed in a deckhouse, which also contained the cabin companionway. As an additional touch of modernity, a searchlight was added to the *Bear's* equipment. The world was changing, and the *Bear* had to change with it.

For the *Bear*, the opening years of the new century were, on the whole, routine, except that in 1912 the vessel assisted in rescue operations when Katmai Volcano on Kodiak Island suddenly erupted, forcing evacuation of the town of Kodiak.

In 1913 the Bear acquired a new skipper, Captain Cochran. He was a good sailor and had a high regard for the ship to which he had been assigned. Under Cochran's command, the *Bear* made her annual journey to Nome and St. Michael.

In 1915, in her forty-second year of service, the *Bear* became an official Coast Guard cutter. That year the former Life Saving Service and the Revenue Cutter Service were joined into a new organization called the United States Coast Guard. It was not really a radical development since both services had been closely cooperating for years. The declaration of war in 1917 had little effect on the operations of the *Bear*. Her paint color was changed from gleaming white to battleship gray. In more southerly waters her gunners were kept ready for possible action against German raiders. As a further wartime precaution, she darkened her lights at night and maintained extra lookouts. Otherwise, World War I did not affect her.

101

Over the years the violent world of the Alaskan frontier had been gradually giving way to a more orderly one. In 1917, for the first time in sixty-five years, no whalers were scheduled to sail for the Arctic. The harshly confining corset, at one time a must for all women, was being abandoned, and whalebone lost its largest market. The once-roaring city of Nome had slowed down considerably. Only a decade before, in 1907, a single beach claim had produced $40,000 in three days' sluicing, bringing Nome's total production to more than $40,000,000. But all that was finished now. The day of the picturesque, easygoing prospector was over. Gold could still be found in Alaska, but it could only be reclaimed by large placer mining operations, requiring large amounts of capital possessed by few men. The heavy passenger traffic by steamer had become a mere trickle, and Nome was just a ghost of the robust mining community it had been a decade earlier.

The same was true to an even greater degree at the once-thriving port of St. Michael. A steady decline in the importance of the Yukon River fur trade was undermining the economy of the area. In time, "St. Mike" too would become a monument to the lusty era of the gold rush. This was saddening to the older hands on the *Bear* who remembered the busy years of the past. Time was rapidly changing the unruly Alaskan frontier into a respectable, law-abiding country, suitable for development by sober-minded men and women bent on establishing

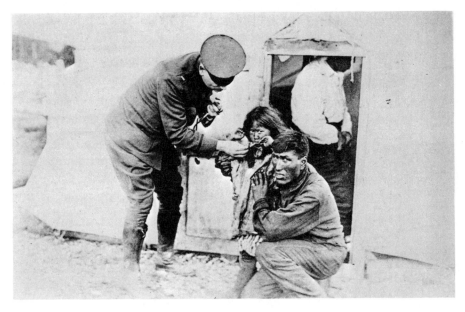

Ship's doctor from the *Bear* taking the temperature of an ailing native child at Unalaska, Alaska.

themselves and their families there. There was no holding back the tide of progress, however nostalgic one might be about the old days.

Life at sea was changing, too. In the days of sail, men on the open sea experienced a sense of adventure and immunity from the affairs of daily living. But in this new world, radio and other improvements in communications were breaking down the barrier between sailors and landlubbers.

In 1919 Captain Preston H. Ubberroth, now skipper of the *Bear,* had his first contact with one of the results of World War I—the Communist government of Soviet Russia.

When the *Bear* visited Siberian villages, her officers ran into new problems created by the new Communist government. Since the United States had not yet extended recognition to the new regime, there were many disputes between American traders and local officials. Many of the latter were attempting to extort high customs duties and trading license fees from merchants.

Occasionally the captain of the *Bear* had to act as mediator between the Soviet government and American citizens. Also to the suspicious and hostile eyes of the Soviet government, the voyages of scientific missions to Alaskan and Siberian waters were regarded as possible violations of Soviet sovereignty. At the time not many persons regarded these brushes with the militant new Russian government as anything more than minor irritations.

The 1920's brought to the United States the era of the so-called Noble Experiment when the federal government sought by official edict to ban the manufacture and sale of alcoholic beverages. This attempt to legislate morality ushered in an era of corruption and lawlessness which benefited no one but the criminal element of society.

The complications created by Prohibition extended all the way to such remote areas as the Big and Little

Diomede Islands. What made the situation especially difficult was that the larger of the islands was Russian and the smaller American. In 1920 the Eskimos had had a very successful whaling season and, like their brethren to the south, were celebrating their success with liberal quantities of homemade liquor. Since Big Diomede (Ratmanov) Island was Russian, the liquor was made there and carried to the smaller island. By the time the *Bear* arrived hardly anyone on Little Diomede was drawing a sober breath. Battles raged all over the island. But the *Bear* soon brought this state of affairs to an end.

The *Bear* was a great, tough ship, but the buffeting of wind and wave was beginning to make inroads on her. During the 1920 cruise, when she was nearing the half-century mark, she ran into a series of troubles that required her to be towed to a major port for repairs. The climax came while she was being towed south of the Aleutians. Suddenly a rough sea lifted the *Bear*'s bow high into the air, breaking the towline. After much difficult maneuvering, another towline was put on the *Bear* and she was brought into Seattle. Careful examination there indicated that her hull had developed several minor leaks and that the original iron fastenings in her timbers were badly rusted. Word quickly circulated that the *Bear* had reached the end of her voyage.

Because of the brutal punishment which the *Bear* had sustained in her long service, naval constructors were ordered to go over her thoroughly. As a result, her leaks were stopped up, and her boiler was repaired. Her skipper of 1916, Captain Cochran, was again ordered to take command. It was under his command, late in January, 1921, that the *Bear* had her moment of truth off the Alaskan coast.

There had been a strong wind, but it had lessened. Yet the sky was still leaden, and the sea was moderate with gray swells. A southeast breeze had been building up from the sea to the coast. By noon it had become a screaming banshee of a wind, measuring 150 miles an hour.

All canvas had been furled, and anything on deck that could give the gale resistance was battened down. Cochran steamed into the storm. In that churning inferno of a sea, the *Bear* pitched and rolled as the waves climbed higher, her aged timbers taking a merciless pounding. High into the sea she rode, coming down with sickening suddenness into the trough. The world was all gray water and screaming wind. It seemed impossible that a small vessel could survive such a battering. Although the crew went about its business, holding to whatever was at hand to stay upright, many doubted that they would survive this storm.

Under the assault of the sea, the *Bear*'s timbers creaked and groaned—but they held together. The old warrior, having taken the worst that the northland could throw against it, was not about to surrender to a gale. To the delight of the crew the old girl was proving that she still

The ship's doctor from the *Bear* checking the health of an Eskimo family at Unalaska, Alaska, during the early 1900's.

had the capacity for taking punishment and surviving. Perhaps they'd live to tell others about this later on.

For hours the *Bear* tossed in the sea. Then the storm abated, and the wind shifted. The heavy gray skies parted to reveal small patches of blue. Nothing had ever looked more beautiful to the tired sailors. Slowly the sea became calm, and the *Bear* was able to resume her course. The old ship, which many had been ready to retire from the service, still had a great deal of life in her. The storm she had ridden out was of such intensity that it had knocked down thousands of trees ashore.

Once again the *Bear* had confounded her critics by

proving that she was far from finished. It was no wonder that in seafaring circles she acquired the reputation of a vessel with a charmed life, impervious to oceanic assault. Nevertheless, she was heading into her final years on the Bering Sea Patrol. The destiny which had taken her on her fantastic career in the northland was running its course. But there were still a few surprises left.

One of the incidents of the *Bear*'s latter years on patrol concerned the renowned explorer Roald Amundsen. It began one day in June, 1921, while the *Bear* was anchored off Nome. On that day Captain Cochran was surprised when Amundsen came to the *Bear* and asked for assistance for his ship, the *Maud*, disabled with a broken propeller off the Siberian coast. Three years before, he had left Norway for the Arctic with the intention of drifting toward the North Pole. After spending three years in the ice to the north of Siberia and slowly working eastward, he had finally been blocked by the ice. He needed help for his imprisoned ship.

In the tradition of his service, Cochran responded to Amundsen's plea. He gave orders that the *Bear* get under way north. Cochran's distinguished passenger gave his host some interesting details on his adventurous career as an Arctic explorer. He explained how in 1906, in his small vessel *Gjöa*, he had struggled for three years in the ice between Greenland and Canada, eventually sailing into the Arctic. His journey had taken him along the northern coast of Alaska, past Point Barrow. Then

(Official U.S. Navy Photograph)

The midnight watch. The U.S. Coast Guard cutter *Bear* in Alaskan waters, June 10, 1924.

he had sailed south through the Bering Strait to Nome, completing the first sea voyage from the Atlantic to the Pacific via the Northwest Passage. Although this northerly route had been previously marked out by earlier explorers, none had been able to negotiate it. In the early phase of the voyage, Amundsen had accurately fixed the position of the North Magnetic Pole, which had been located only approximately by the British explorer Sir James Ross.

The Bear, going to the aid of the *Maud,* picked her up off the Siberian coast. When Amundsen's ship was clear of St. Lawrence Island, Cochran provided the explorer with charts of the passes through the Aleutians and put him back on the *Maud.* Another mission had been accomplished.

109

On his return to San Francisco, Cochran learned that his winter headquarters had been changed from San Diego to Oakland. He was also ordered to repaint the *Bear* to a gleaming white, her former color.

All about the San Francisco waterfront were melancholy reminders of a changing seafaring world. Tied to the dock were many whaling vessels, rotting away. Even the once brawling saloons along the waterfront had become tame and respectable.

The *Bear*, however, was far from idle. She ran surveys in remote places; laws prohibiting the sale of liquor to Eskimos were strictly enforced; Eskimos were punished for permitting their dogs to kill reindeer. The *Bear* was in the forefront of the newly recognized science of oceanography, conducting experiments of her own and assisting scientific expeditions in carrying out their projects. As always, she carried an assortment of humanity to and from points in the north.

Late in 1922 the *Bear* steamed north from Unalaska toward Nome. It was a clear day, and indications were that it would be an easy sail. The picture changed suddenly toward evening, when a heavy fog settled down and a sharp drop in temperature warned of an approaching ice pack. The next morning Cochran found that his ship was completely locked in ice—and she might stay there until the following summer. It was a dismal prospect.

After reporting the situation by radio, Cochran took

The *Bear* anchored in the ice off Point Barrow, Alaska, August, 1922, during one of her annual patrols to the Arctic.

all necessary steps to prepare for a retreat over the ice. He put a supply of food and supplies on the ice and packed all official papers and records.

When the news gradually reached the States, an angry chorus of protest began concerning the *Bear* and her supposedly unseaworthy state. Most of the critics had little knowledge either of the ship or of the north. But it was a tempting topic for editorial writers, who thundered about the approaching end of a great ship.

None of the editorial furor was of much help to Captain Cochran and his crew, however. They went calmly about their business, taking their regular watches on the ice and waiting for an opportunity to move their vessel out of the pack. For forty-two anxious days they waited.

Then, as suddenly as it had locked the *Bear* in, the ice pack quickly moved away from her. Through skillful use of sail and a damaged screw propeller, Cochran worked the *Bear* into open sea.

The ship which had nearly been counted out made another miraculous recovery and returned to San Francisco under sail. This time, however, members of Congress had noted the incident, and there was considerable criticism of permitting a ship of the *Bear*'s age to remain in Arctic service. The upshot was that funds were appropriated for a new cutter, the *Northland,* to take the *Bear*'s place. Even the old vessel's friends could see that her long saga in the north was running its course.

The Treasury Department, in its annual report for 1927, wrote what it considered to be the *Bear*'s epitaph:

Her duties in the service for many years have sent her annually to the faraway North on cruises to Alaska and the Arctic Ocean and to Point Barrow. Her yearly visits to the northern country have been a welcome episode in the lives of the natives. Her coming among them was an inspiration, a promise always fulfilled, a light penetrating the darkness and wilderness of their desolation. Her mission was to help, to aid, to succor, and she fulfilled that mission. Her record is both conspicuous and interesting. She was always ready, exemplifying the motto

(Official U.S. Coast Guard Photograph)

The *Bear* trapped in ice off Alaska in 1922. She was the first vessel acquired by the Coast Guard designed for navigation through ocean ice.

of the service. Returning to the States from a 6-months' cruise in Arctic waters, she set out again on November 27, 1897, just three weeks from the time of her arrival from the North on the historical expedition for the relief of the whaling fleet caught in the ice in the vicinity of Point Barrow, and 10 months later, she returned bringing four crews of wrecked whalers without loss or accident of any kind. She is 53 years old and for more than 40 years has valiantly borne the rigors of the hardest of service, battling oftentimes with the northern ice that threatened to send her to her doom. The ravages of service and time have at last told on her. Her work is done. Her last cruise to the frozen regions of the North is made and she must go to the inactive list. This old ship will have a place always in the hearts of her shipmates and in the history of the service.

They were eloquent words, but only partially true. It was true that the *Bear* had come to the end of her long Arctic service. But to say that she was ready for the scrap heap was a bit premature. There was a good deal more life left in the old ship than the Treasury Department knew. She would outlive her epitaph by more than thirty years.

The Treasury writer might also have noted that during her long career on patrol, the *Bear* had departed for Point Barrow thirty-four times. On all but four of these trips she had succeeded in pushing through the ice. With the exception of the *Corwin,* which had visited Point Barrow in 1880, no other cutter had succeeded in reaching this northernmost point of Alaska.

The reindeer which Mike Healy and Dr. Jackson had so farsightedly imported from Siberia had increased enormously to almost 1,000,000 head. Increased knowledge of sanitation and medicine brought to the Eskimos by doctors carried by the *Bear* had greatly reduced the incidence of disease and epidemics. In part because of the work of the ship and other members of the patrol, Alaska's fur farms, fishing industry, and canneries were

The *Bear* under way in northern waters. A painting by Charles Robert Patterson.

thriving, and the sealeries were flourishing. In the years that the *Bear* had been on patrol, hundreds of millions of dollars in gold and natural products had come from what was formerly considered an unproductive northern wasteland. The legacy of the *Bear* to the nation which it served was a great one.

As an accolade for her many successful journeys to the

north, the *Bear* on her last voyage south from Point Barrow picked up Sir Hubert Wilkins, the noted explorer, for transportation home. Sir Hubert had become a world-famous authority on the north in the years since he had first seen the *Bear* in 1912 on a photography expedition near Point Barrow, Alaska.

On her return to San Francisco, the vessel lay alongside the pier at the Coast Guard base at Government Island. Soon the orders would come through officially terminating her service on the patrol. As she moved into the beautiful harbor at the end of the voyage, the men of the *Bear* could see her replacement, *Northland.* It was a poignant moment for all hands, especially the older ones. For Captain Cochran who had spent so much of his career on the proud old ship, the leave-taking must have been painful.

A last muster was held on the deck of the old ship as she lay at anchor on the bay. To the melancholy shrill of the bos'n's pipe, the commission pennant came down slowly. It was captured by the quartermaster before it could hit the deck and given to Captain Cochran—something for him to cherish as long as he lived.

The final entries were made in the log, the officers removed all their personal belongings. Captain Cochran left his command to start a three-year tour of duty as commander of the Bering Sea Patrol with headquarters in Unalaska. Quiet and silent as a tomb, the old ship lay alongside the dock.

The *Bear* in polar waters. This painting was done for the Coast Guard
by Hunter Wood.

8

To the Bottom of the World

The *Bear* seemed doomed to end her days as a dead hulk moored to the Coast Guard base at Oakland. What would happen to this great ship of the northland? Would she have to suffer the final ignominy of being sold for scrap?

For three years she lay at the dock at Oakland. Then, when it appeared that her time had run out, the people of Oakland came to her rescue. Seafaring men of Oakland and other lovers of the sea and its lore were determined to buy her and preserve her as a museum ship. Under an act of Congress of February 2, 1929, she was decommissioned and placed out of service in May and sold to the city of Oakland. It was not the worst fate that could have befallen her. As a marine museum the *Bear* would at least be a reminder to those who visited her of the epic of American exploration in the Arctic.

The city of Oakland treated the *Bear* well. It kept her paint a gleaming white, and all her gear was as shipshape as ever. Tourists by the thousands came on board, staring at her rigging and asking questions about what she had done and where she had been. For a time the *Bear* even achieved fame as a motion-picture celebrity. The Fox Film Company thought that she would be ideal for their version of Jack London's novel *The Sea Wolf,* dealing with sealing in the days of sail.

Then came the Great Depression—and the *Bear* was caught in its trough. Her custodial crew which drew a meager salary from the city of Oakland was removed. For a short time, Sea Scouts looked after her and then were succeeded by two paid employees. Surely the career of the famed ship had ended.

But then a great adventurer entered her saga. He was Rear Admiral Richard E. Byrd, the explorer. He had been the first to fly over the North Pole and one of the first to fly across the Atlantic. In 1928 he had conducted his first exploration of the Antarctic. In 1932 he was planning his second expedition when the *Bear* was suggested to him as a possible member of the expedition.

The idea appealed to Byrd, who sent representatives to examine the ship. In their opinion, the *Bear* was fit to enter the ice again. Aside from his romantic feeling about the old ship, Byrd was feeling the effects of the Depression. He needed a good ship at a reasonable price, and the *Bear* met those requirements.

City regulations required that the ship be sold at public auction. The proceeding was to be merely a legal formality. However, on the day of the auction, a local junkman startled everyone by starting the bidding with an offer of $1,000. It almost broke up the auction. But as Byrd said, "Somebody spoke firmly but discreetly to the junkman. At any rate, it was his first and last bid." The *Bear* was sold to Byrd for the very reasonable price of $1,050, and she was rechristened *Bear of Oakland* in token of Byrd's gratitude.

Again a new life was about to begin for a ship which had seemed ready for oblivion. Again the *Bear* had displayed a miraculous capacity for recovering from a seemingly hopeless situation. After spending more than half a century in the ice of northern seas, she was about to penetrate the secrets of the immense continent at the bottom of the world.

Soon after the vessel was sold to the admiral, she was sailed to Boston by a volunteer crew, being eventually joined by the *Jacob Ruppert*, named after the brewing magnate who generously helped finance the expedition. For the first time in more than forty years, the *Bear* was back in Atlantic waters, where she had begun her illustrious career.

Both vessels required extensive overhaul, and the problem was how to effect this with the limited funds at Byrd's disposal. The solution came in the form of volunteer labor. Men donated their services without cost to be part of what they considered a historic under-

The *Bear* as she appeared following her return in 1935 from an Antarctic expedition with Rear Admiral Richard E. Byrd, USN. The vessel was purchased by Byrd in 1932 and refitted at the Boston Navy Yard.

Small stores being loaded aboard the *Bear of Oakland* (formerly the revenue cutter *Bear*) on August 25, 1933, prior to departure for Little America with Admiral Byrd.

taking. Others of Byrd's needs were supplied by industrial firms which provided aircraft, tractors, and other material.

In September, 1933, the *Bear* left Boston under the command of Lieutenant Robert A. J. English, USN. Bostonians lined the waterfront, cheering the great old ship as she left on her Antarctic quest. The *Ruppert*, being a faster ship, moved out on October 11.

Byrd's general plan called for passage through the Panama Canal and on into the South Pacific Ocean. The *Bear*'s voyage to southern seas did not begin auspiciously, however. On the way to Panama, she ran into a hurricane and narrowly missed foundering off Southport, North Carolina. Her commander, Lieutenant English, tried to reach Southport Harbor. Heavy seas were breaking over the decks, and the ship was taking water through the hatches and companionways. Although the men pumped frantically, they couldn't keep pace with the flooding. Time after time the engineers crawled into the bilges, trying to scrape away coagulated coal from the strainers. It was in vain. The coating had become too thick. Finally, the steam pumps stalled for want of suction, and the hand pumps were no match for the fury of the sea. The water level rose sharply in the engine room. To save the shaft bearings, the engine was stopped. Although there was no dry coal, the engineers managed to keep the fires going for several hours.

In spite of heroic efforts, the water kept gaining. Then all power and lights failed. Sails close-hauled, the ship pushed toward Frying Pan Shoals Lightship. After what seemed an eternity, but which in reality was only several hours, the *Bear* was able to reach the entrance to Southport Harbor. The largely amateur crew had acquitted itself well in its first real trial. The old *Bear* had come safely through the ordeal too. Nevertheless, because of the punishment she had taken, it was necessary for her to return to Newport News for drydocking.

On October 22 the *Bear's* sister ship, *Ruppert,* took aboard planes and other gear and started for the Panama Canal and the South Pacific. The *Bear* followed the *Ruppert* on November 1. Both ships were to rendezvous in the Bay of Whales in Antarctica three months later.

At Wellington and Dunedin, New Zealand, the *Bear* took on additional supplies for the expedition, increasing her deck load substantially. At Dunedin, radiograms were received from Byrd that the *Jacob Ruppert* had reached Little America. Byrd had made exploration flights along the Antarctic coast and was having considerable difficulty in landing provisions. The trip south had revealed hidden weaknesses in the *Ruppert's* old engines. Lieutenant English detected a note of urgency in the messages. It was obvious that the *Bear's* help was needed quickly to solve the problems that lay ahead.

English took steps to speed the loading of the *Bear* while he studied his charts. He could see that the Bay of Whales, on which Little America was located, was an opening in the Ross Sea. The sea itself was a huge indentation in the Antarctic ice shelf. Along the entire circumference of the bay the edges were constantly crumbling, filling it with huge bergs, most of them far greater than those found in Arctic waters. Some were so large that an entire day could be spent in passing them.

The continuous calving of bergs was making it hard for the *Ruppert* to remain at her moorings. Besides, she was inadequately armored for the heavy assaults of Antarctic ice. Her plates were only about seven-eighths of an inch thick and rusted. She did not offer much security. Radio information arriving later informed English that the *Ruppert* might not be able to land the Byrd party before the winter set in. It was especially hazardous for a steel ship to stay much longer in the Bay of Whales, for the intense cold could make her hull so brittle that it would lose resiliency and crack. It was a race against time for English to arrive at the rendezvous to assist the landing and to allow the *Ruppert* to move out of the Bay of Whales. The speed at which he could move the *Bear* to the prearranged point held the key to success or failure.

On the clear, cold night of January 31, 1934, the *Bear* rounded the white tower of West Cape and steamed down the Bay of Whales. The sea was bathed in the yellow haze of the midnight sun at the bottom of the world.

To the men on the *Ruppert,* the arrival of the *Bear* was the reassurance they had long awaited. As the ship came within hailing distance, the *Ruppert* gave her three welcoming blasts on the whistle. Lieutenant English responded by smartly breaking out three signal flags which had already been hoisted in stops. The three flags meant in Navy language that the *Bear* and her men were fit for duty. She had made the 2,500-mile run from Dunedin, New Zealand, to the Bay of Whales in twelve days—not bad for a ship which had almost been consigned to the scrap pile.

The crews of both ships pitched into the difficult task of unloading stores from the ships. Tons of supplies and equipment had to be moved across the treacherous pressure ridges and into the camp at Little America.

As the men worked unloading ships' stores, they learned something of the nature of the forbidding land in which they were to spend the next months. What they found out was not reassuring. This was a continent still in the grip of the ice age. The bleak, high, barren mountain ranges, the howling winds, and the absence of any life except for a few whales, seals, and penguins defied man.

Two days after the *Bear* had arrived, the *Jacob Ruppert* completed transferring coal and set sail for New Zealand. She took with her the surgeon of the expedition, who had become ill.

As Admiral Byrd surveyed the headquarters of his original expedition to Little America, he was amazed to find that much of the food left over from the former expedition was still fresh. Many items of considerable value were salvaged and later put to use. In the food caches alone he found two and one-half tons of flour, several hundred pounds of butter, large amounts of condensed and evaporated milk, canned meats, fruit, fish, preserves and other foods. Also in a good state of preservation were coal, gasoline, kerosene, lubricating oils, medical supplies, radio equipment, aviation tools, photographic equipment, and similar items.

Other members of the expedition had dug down to the airplanes used on the earlier voyage, which had been anchored on a ridge to the eastward. The planes were entirely buried, but searchers examined the aircraft and reported them in good condition.

The *Bear* left the Bay of Whales on February 5, flying Admiral Byrd's pennant, with her first objective to explore the coast of King Edward VII Land to the east. In all the history of Antarctic exploration only four ships had penetrated into that area. They had accomplished little, however, because of the heavy ice pack. Byrd hoped to press the investigation to a more successful conclusion.

The cruise of the *Bear* deeply impressed the admiral with her staying qualities. He found "joy and spirit to the *Bear's* attack which were lacking in the *Ruppert's*. The *Bear* was a wooden ship; she was built for ice. She could hit with both hands where the flimsy *Ruppert* had to wheedle and cajole; she could lower her head and bore in where the *Ruppert* had to turn tail and seek a better 'ole. Therein lay the merit of the honorable and ancient *Bear of Oakland*. And she was worked by a smart crew, too, disciplined, keen, and loyal to her officers."

The first objective of Lieutenant English, as skipper of the *Bear,* was Cape Colbeck. To portside on the voyage was the Great Ice Barrier, rising steeply from the sea to a height of 150 feet in some places. The sea was rough, and the winds rose to 40 knots while the *Bear* rolled and pitched heavily.

As the ship approached Cape Colbeck, she ran into an extensive unbroken field of ice. Skirting it, she headed toward Biscoe Bay. It was only the beginning of a series of problems, however. About 25 miles northeast of Colbeck a line of huge icebergs blocked the *Bear's* path. The bergs were so close together that it seemed impossible to pass. Soundings at five-minute intervals indicated that the bergs were aground. Apparently the ship was above a submerged ridge covered by 45 fathoms of water. They had found the underwater extension of the Alexandra Mountains of King Edward VII Land.

In her third day out of Little America, the *Bear* had sailed farther east than any previous Antarctic voyagers. She had entered an unknown region, becoming the first United States vessel to penetrate new areas of the Antarctic in three-quarters of a century. It was work of the most rugged kind. Stubbornly the explorers pushed into ice 40 feet thick. Unsuccessfully, they hunted north and south for a more favorable passage. Then suddenly the *Bear* found herself caught in the ice pack. It was real trouble again.

Only one man had the experience and the skill needed to extricate the *Bear* from the pack. He was the ice pilot,

Captain Bendick Johansen, who had to find a small area into which the *Bear* could smash her bulk. His eyes narrowed as he scanned the bleak horizon. At last he found what he was looking for.

With barely enough room to maneuver and move quickly, the *Bear* plunged ahead. Her effort was rewarded by a small gap in the ice field. She backed off and again drove into the ice at full speed. Eventually she broke through. Now the way was open to Little America and the Bay of Whales.

Back at Little America, Byrd found that his crew had accomplished near miracles in setting up the new headquarters for the expedition. At this remote and southernmost part of the world, a village had sprung up, equipped with electric light and power, a complete broadcasting and field communications plant, a well-equipped aviation service with 4 planes and skilled personnel, machine shops, four tractors, nearly 150 dogs, a first-class meteorological station, a dairy plant with 4 head of cattle, and medical facilities. There were also a scientific staff and laboratory equipped to delve into twenty-two branches of science, a fully stocked galley, a library, a meteor observatory, and a motion-picture theater wired for sound. It was the most ambitious and successful undertaking ever carried out in the South Polar region.

Byrd's pleasure in what he saw was short-lived, however. His trained eye had noticed that the sheet of ice on which Little America was located was definitely sepa-

View from the foredeck, looking aft toward the bridge, of the *Bear* while she was being refitted for the United States Antarctic Expedition, 1939–41.

rated from the main barrier mass. The widening cracks and the movement of the ice on the swell foreshadowed possible disaster. It was entirely possible that the headquarters built with so much labor and care could suddenly find itself calved off from the main body of ice and pulled out to sea. Byrd had always been aware of this possibility. Now it looked as though it might actually happen.

He called together the senior members of the expedition and discussed the situation with them. As a precautionary measure it was agreed that a reserve cache of supplies be established on the high barrier about a mile southeast of Little America. This was the highest ground immediately within reach and seemed the area most likely to survive a sudden movement of ice.

Practically all the energies and resources of the expedition were thrown into the difficult task of setting up an alternative headquarters. The sailmakers of the *Bear* were put to work sewing tents, windproof clothing, medical kits, and related items. By almost ceaseless effort over a two-week period the camp was completed.

On February 18 the *Bear* left the Bay of Whales to rendezvous with *Discovery II*, a British explorer ship. In the Ross Sea she ran into endless fields of pancake ice and squalls, indicative of coming winter. Squalls deepened into a heavy snowstorm. Visibility was nearly zero. Yet the old ship pushed her way to the rendezvous. In the evening of February 21 the ships met at the northern edge of the ice pack, about 400 miles above Little America. On Board the *Discovery II* was a new medical officer to replace the ailing doctor previously with the expedition. Through first-rate seamanship the vessels were brought alongside each other in the storm, and the new doctor came on board the *Bear*.

In addition to the new medical officer, the *Discovery II* transferred to the *Bear* 6 tons of food and general supplies and 3,000 gallons of gasoline. On the evening of the day that the *Bear* headed south for the Bay of Whales, the sun set for the first time. Byrd described it as "a gorgeous burst of florid flame in a white chalice, long shadows reaching in the lee of every raised thing, and the opposite sky trembling with delicate rose-colored lights."

At Little America on February 23, the temperature had dropped to 24° below zero. A four-inch layer of ice sealed the Bay of Whales. This made it necessary for

Byrd to search for a possible mooring place in the event that freezing of the bay deprived the *Bear* of her former berth.

While Byrd was anxiously awaiting word of the vessel's progress, the old ship was having a very rough time. Considering that the very future of the expedition hung in the balance, it is easy to understand Byrd's concern. His worries were not eased when he received a radio message from Lieutenant English on February 23 which read:

From 0300 to 0600 (3:00 until 6:00 A.M.) fought way south foot at a time with ship giving utmost for a distance of three miles through very hard, newly-frozen close pack. We are twenty miles from Bay of Whales by DR (dead reckoning). Visibility poor, sky overcast, air temperature plus two degrees. At 0630 ice over six inches thick, no leads visible, nothing but one solid sheet as far as can be seen in all directions except thin dark pencil of wake which is also rapidly freezing.

This discouraging information was followed a few minutes later by an even more somber message which advised that the ship:

had stopped dead and was unable to make another foot in this direction. I am endeavoring to get steerage way and on a northerly heading so as to fight way to open water in that direction. Johansen states this ice much worse than that experienced in 1929 and believes no ship could penetrate it. Pack is so heavy and widespread that I doubt if anything less than a northerly gale could break it up, and a gale from that direction would be hazardous to this ship. This command is unwilling to give up the attainment of any assigned mission, yet it is humanly impossible to get a ship beyond our farthest south.

The message produced a mood of despondency at Little America. All the elements of a disaster were present. If the *Bear* were trapped in the ice, the chances were her men might not survive the rigors of an Antarctic winter. Little America was overcrowded with men scheduled to return on her. Also, the doctor on the *Bear* was urgently needed. The men planning to return to New Zealand on the ship left off their packing. The odds were fairly high that they might not leave at all.

Nevertheless, one could not remain passive in the face of disaster. Byrd asked a pilot to prepare the autogyro for flight. The vehicle was dug out of the drift and warmed up. Byrd and the pilot took off on a reconnaissance of the bay. By flying low through the sea smoke across the mouth of the bay, they saw tide rips had opened the ice along the barrier. If the *Bear* could somehow free herself from her present position, she would be able to get through to the camp.

Encouraged by the news that the path to the bay was open, English renewed his efforts to punch his way out of the ice. The ice was now adhesive and rubbery, bending rather than splitting at the ship's impact. Never had the old vessel had a meaner adversary. Every ounce of her weight had to be brought into action against this pack. Doggedly, foot by foot, she advanced, all her crewmen praying that the old ship would get them through. At midnight Byrd received the glad tidings that the gallant *Bear* had made it once more. She had vanquished the bitterest foe she had encountered in her long battle with ice. The expedition had been reprieved at the last minute.

The number of men greeting the *Bear* on her return to the Bay of Whales was small, but it was probably the most enthusiastic crowd in her career.

Within a short time after anchoring at Little America, the new doctor was landed. Not long afterward he performed an emergency appendectomy which saved the life of a member of the party. Exactly eight hours later the *Bear* was ready to get under way for the trip north to New Zealand. Her departure was sad for men who had worked closely together. Those staying watched as her masts gradually became tiny specks on the horizon and then disappeared altogether.

By noon Lieutenant English was pushing through the Ross Sea, with the ship's engines open wide and every inch of canvas spread to take advantage of the winds. She had several close calls in the Bay of Whales, narrowly missing crashing into the barrier, but she finally gained the open sea, which was filled with gigantic drifting icebergs.

The *Bear* made good progress north in spite of ice

floes, gales, and shrieking winds. March gales sped her
on her way, and it was a southerly gale which blew her
out of the Ross Sea. On March 2 the gale became a hurricane, and the *Bear* had to heave to until the terrible wind
diminished. Later that day the hurricane moderated to
a gale. Setting the lower topsails and stopping the engines, English let the gale bear him along. The following
day another hurricane struck. The vessel labored in
mountainous green seas, rolling 50 degrees on each side,
until she was almost on beam's end. She seemed like a
toy in the hands of monstrous forces which could at any
time destroy her. But nine days later she reached Dunedin after perhaps the stormiest passage ever made in the
Antarctic. Any way one looked at it, "it was a magnificent
season's work for a ship supposedly tardy at the grave-
yard," as Byrd put it. She had made six transits of the
Ross Sea, exploring 40,000 square miles of unknown seas.
Six lines of soundings had been made and various hydro-
graphic stations established.

Her work at Little America temporarily over, the *Bear*
rejoined the *Jacob Ruppert* for the winter layover at
Dunedin. During those months of waiting she underwent
extensive overhaul. She received a new jib boom and a
new mainmast and was also calked and repainted.

January, 1935, found the *Bear* heading south once
more toward the Ross Sea. This time her voyage was
easy, for the sea was unusually free of ice. On her way
from Dunedin the ship took a line of soundings, sailing
directly to the coast of South Victoria Land.

(The National Archives)

The *Bear's* second figurehead, installed at the time of her refitting for the Antarctic Expedition, 1939. The original figurehead was removed and given to the Mariners Museum, Newport News, Virginia.

On the night of January 15 the *Bear* ran into a blizzard, and the thermometer fell sharply. By the next morning the air had cleared, and Franklin Island could be seen. Around noon English had reached the vicinity of Cape Bird and Beaufort Island. As if to repay the old vessel for the rigors of the past year, the Antarctic presented English and his crew with one of the most magnificent views in the world: the great volcanoes of Ross Island—Erebus, Terror, Bird, and Terra Nova. Mount Erebus, an active volcano, stood at the gateway of the barrier, with glaciers threading their way down its sides and vapor rising from its cone.

English had long been intrigued by the oceanography of the barrier. The movement of the Ross Ice Barrier, as well as its structure, had been a mystery to scientists. Opinion was divided on whether it was retreating or receding and whether the quantities of ice pushing out through the glaciers from the interior plateaus more than compensated for the loss at the edge resulting from the calving of icebergs. The barrier had been surveyed only twice since its discovery and charting by Ross in 1841. For the 1935 survey, Lieutenant English was equipped with the latest scientific instruments. They included a gyro compass, pelorus, range finder, records, and similar apparatus.

From the very beginning of his survey, he found evidence of great changes had occurred since the survey made in 1911 by Lieutenant H. L. L. Pennell of the Royal Navy, a member of the expedition led by Captain Robert F. Scott, also of the Royal Navy. Throughout the first 150 miles of the western reaches of the barrier he found the edge 13.8 miles north of the position fixed in 1911. The entire aspect and contour of front had gradually changed since the Pennell investigation. This extension was confirmed all the way from Cape Crozier to West Cape—a distance of 460 miles. According to English's calculations, the average annual rate of movement was ½ mile. This totaled an accumulation of 6,348 square miles of ice in twenty-four years. It was an important discovery.

On the afternoon of January 18, English entered Dis-

Photo of the *Bear* in the Antarctic as part of the United States Antarctic Expedition.

covery Inlet and radioed Little America he would reach the Bay of Whales the following morning.

At expedition headquarters in Little America, Byrd and his aides had for weeks been considering the problem of evacuation and reloading men and provisions, preparatory to departure from the Antarctic. Byrd had been in regular communication with the ships. Tractors and dog teams had been steadily moving stores to a cache. The dog crates were ripped out of the caved-in tunnels and piled on the surface for transfer to the *Ruppert*. Reloading of the vast store of equipment and provisions on the vessels would be at least as difficult as the loading had been—perhaps more so.

While Byrd was anxiously awaiting the arrival of the *Ruppert*, the *Bear* was being roughed by onrushes of ice. Five times she was driven from her berth. Once driven out by a gale, seven days passed before she could find a berth. What had happened to the *Ruppert*?

The answer was that she had sailed into a solid pack just north of the Ross Sea and had been compelled to steer west before she broke through to open sea on January 24. Much to Byrd's relief, she arrived at the Bay of Whales two days later on January 26. It had been a wretched period for Byrd and his men. Rather than risk fatally injuring the steel-hulled *Ruppert*, he decided to keep her farther out to sea and to use the *Bear* as a ferry between the shore and the flagship. Once more, as Byrd said, he "had to rely on the *Bear's* ancient hull," which had never failed him.

To accomplish the project, however, it would be necessary for the *Bear* to come in closer to the camp. On January 26, only a few hours before the *Ruppert* arrived, the ice pilot, Captain Johansen, had tried to drive the *Bear* into Eleanor Bolling Bight, but he was repulsed by the ice. On the thirtieth, he decided to have another go at it. English radioed that he was going to attempt to enter

The *Bear* at the Bay of Whales, Antarctic, during the United States Antarctic Expedition. This photo shows the vessel after she had been converted to diesel power and otherwise modernized.

the bight. All went well at first, with the *Bear* managing to anchor to ice at the head of the bight. The reloading was proceeding smoothly when almost without warning, 50 feet of the barrier broke out alongside the ship. Like a wounded animal, the *Bear* groaned, lay over for a short time until the weight of the ice eased, then slowly righted herself.

The incredible ship had survived a blow which would have been fatal to the *Ruppert*. Without her the expedition would have come to disaster. Byrd's judgment of the vessel had been sound. Now his admiration for her was greater than ever. At last the loading was finished and with some nostalgia Byrd made his departure from Little America. It had been a very successful expedition. He had brought great credit to himself and to his country. The *Bear* had been a very important factor in his achievement. He made what he thought was a valedictory statement on her services, praising "her last polar" voyage.

By the mid-thirties the character of polar exploration was changing. In the early days, voyages to the Antarctic had been primarily private scientific ventures. However, in the years since World War I there had been a rising tide of nationalism. Exploration of the continent at the bottom of the world was becoming increasingly a mark of national prestige. There was also the possibility that eventually mineral riches would be found within its icy depths. There was speculation, too, about the military usefulness of the Antarctic.

In 1939 the United States Antarctic Service was established, and Byrd was named to lead a third expedition to Antarctica. President Franklin D. Roosevelt, who appointed Byrd to head the expedition, made it clear that the admiral was not to winter in the Antarctic. His mission was to set up bases and instruct members of the expedition in their tasks before returning. The expedition's primary function was to examine the area from Alexander I Island to Edward VII Peninsula.

Although Congress voted Byrd $677,000 for his venture, it was not enough. An additional $240,000 was contributed by Byrd and his associates. At the time, Byrd was the owner of the *Bear*. The other vessel of his new two-ship fleet was the *North Star*, which had been working in Alaskan waters. She was a large cargo carrier, well suited to the needs of transporting planes and other heavy equipment. In command of the *Bear* was Lieutenant Richard Cruzen. On this expedition the *Bear* was Byrd's flagship. To ready her for her trip south, her power plant was completely overhauled, her double-expansion engine removed and a power diesel engine installed. The coal bunkers, antique Scots boiler, and noisy steam power plant were taken out. She now had electric generators, and her power plant was as modern as that on any other ship.

For the third time she entered the Bay of Whales after a good voyage south. Byrd had always wanted to explore the coast of Marie Byrd Land east of the Bay of Whales. But he had not been able to do so on previous expeditions. Now he could carry out his cherished ambition. The *Bear* sailed eastward from the bay with a seaplane on deck for exploratory flights. Exploration, however, was only one of Byrd's motives in sailing east. He also wanted to set up a base on Charcot Island. This would be the East Base and the counterpart of the West Base at Little America. He would put wintering parties at both ends of the coastline in which the United States had territorial interest.

The always unpredictable ice prevented Byrd from making a landing on Charcot Island. Therefore, he sailed farther east to Marguerite Bay, where he sighted an unknown island, which he named Stonington Island. It would serve as the site for the East Base. The wintering parties established on the bases turned out to be very productive, undertaking extensive reconnaissance flights and sledge journeys and gathering much valuable scientific information.

In the spring of 1941 the *Bear* headed back home. In the white eternal vastness of the Antarctic the events of the world up north didn't seem too important. Nevertheless, the world was pressing in on the *Bear* and its crew. World War II had already been under way for two years.

If any members of the crew of the *Bear* were looking forward to quiet days of rest and recuperation from the hardships of the Antarctic, they were mistaken. Before long both they and their ship would be involved in the tragic events which were shaping the history of the world.

9

A Warrior Ship Stands Guard

When the *Bear* returned home from the Antarctic, the United States was not yet involved in World War II. But many of its leaders were sure war was coming.

The shipping routes to Europe lay through some of the roughest waters in the world, off the coast of Greenland. Control of the waters off Greenland was important for another reason. It was situated in the region where Europe's "weather was made" and therefore extremely useful for weather prediction. The Germans were well aware of this and, shortly after their occupation of Norway and Denmark, had set up weather and intelligence units on the island. This posed a great peril to the vital North Atlantic shipping route. From their position on Greenland the Germans could direct submarine strikes against convoys passing through adjacent waters.

The United States was also acutely aware of the value of Greenland in the North Atlantic war and had negotiated an agreement with the Danish government in exile to enter Greenland and search for evidence of German intelligence operations and take such action as might be necessary. It was also imperative to maintain a constant patrol of Greenland waters to protect Allied shipping in that area. The big problem now was to find ships for the job.

Coast Guard Commandant Admiral Russell R. Waesche was searching for suitable cutters. Since the Coast Guard had been maintaining the International Ice Patrol in the North Atlantic, as well as other far northern operations, it was logical that it take over the contemplated patrol. Coast Guard cutters had been performing this duty since 1914 to protect shipping against floating icebergs in the much-traveled North Atlantic shipping lanes. The major difference, however, between the Ice Patrol and the one now under consideration was that the latter operation would have to be on a year-round basis.

It would be a rugged job. Calm days are almost unknown in those waters. Duty would be hard on crews and ships. It would take specially designed and equipped vessels to handle this assignment. In casting about for ships, Admiral Waesche remembered the *Bear*. True, she was an old ship, yet a very tough one and ideally suited to northern patrols. The trouble was she no longer belonged to the Coast Guard, but was the property of Admiral Byrd. Thus began a protracted correspondence between Byrd and Waesche. Byrd was reluctant to part with the vessel, to which he had become attached. But ultimately he turned her over the Coast Guard.

The vessel received by the Coast Guard was greatly modified from the earlier cutter. Byrd and the Navy had invested considerable sums in her to bring her up to date. Now the last trace of her sailing days was removed. Her masts were cut down, her sails discarded. The Coast Guard installed three rapid-firing guns. An amphibian plane, carrying bombs, was put on her deck. For protective coloration she was painted white to match the ice. She carried a larger crew to permit the landing of armed parties when necessary. Her skipper was Lieutenant Peter J. Neimo, USCG, who had served on her in the Antarctic. The cutter which left Boston Harbor on July 2, 1941, was very different from the ship which had sailed under Mike Healy. Most of the men who had served on her in those bygone days were now dead or were very old.

The waters patrolled by the *Bear* and her sister ships on "Neutrality Patrol" were well known to the Germans who were operating there in considerable numbers. Most of the charts of the area had been in the possession of the Danish government in Copenhagen. With the occupation of Denmark by the Germans, they fell into the possession of the enemy. That meant the *Bear* would have to assist in the preparation of a new set of charts. Uncharted areas would have to be surveyed and recorded. In reconnoitering the fjords, the cutters sailed up one side and then came down on the other to make the soundings.

What made the task even more difficult was the absence of aids to navigation. Since it had been the policy of the Danish government to isolate Greenland to protect the native way of life, the only navigators were local seamen. Coast Guardsmen would have to spend many a weary hour keeping open the convoy routes for vessels and the air routes for planes—breaking ice, finding leads, fighting off submarines, rescuing survivors, maintaining aids to navigation, transporting men and supplies, reporting weather and ice conditions—and above all, maintaining continuous patrols.

Getting the patrol under way took some time. For the first few weeks there was little action. The situation changed drastically, however, on September 4, 1941, when a German submarine sank the USS *Geer* while she was carrying mail to Greenland. The war was now at our very doorstep. It was no longer a faraway conflict in nations across the broad Atlantic, but one which now involved American men and ships. Public indignation at the sinking of the *Geer* was high. Reflecting this feeling, President Roosevelt on September 12 issued a blunt warning to the Axis powers to keep out of American waters or suffer the consequences. It was obvious to everyone that the United States could not continue to remain neutral for much longer.

At this fateful moment in our history an innocent-looking fishing vessel was sighted by ships of the patrol.

(The National Archives)

Following her service with the U.S. Antarctic Expedition, the *Bear* was again refitted, this time for service with the Greenland Patrol. This photo shows how the vessel appeared in 1941.

(Official U.S. Coast Guard Photograph)

The *Bear*'s appearance was again changed during her patrol service. This view shows the ship as she finally appeared during World War II.

Members of a sledge party had informed the patrol commander earlier of a party seen landing in a lonely fjord. Routinely, the commander stopped the fishing vessel and sent out a boarding party which sailed her into McKenzie Bay to inspect her.

From the moment that Coast Guardsmen set foot on the vessel they could sense something strange about it. In response to questioning, the twenty-seven persons on board—most of them Danish hunters and Norwegian trappers—claimed to be on a fishing and hunting party. The leader of the expedition was a scientist, and the one woman on board said she was a nurse. On the surface there appeared to be nothing unusual about the party. Nevertheless the Coast Guardsmen remained wary.

When a Coast Guard officer asked, "Have you dropped off any men?" everyone on board answered: "No." But the questioning was persistent, and eventually the people on the fishing vessel realized that their interrogators could not be put off. One of the crew gave the information that two sets of "hunters" had been dropped off, one with radio equipment, about 500 miles north of the present location. They identified the ship as the Norwegian trawler *Buskoe*. She had been seized by the Germans and was being used to service a radio station in Greenland.

Commander Edward H. Smith immediately ordered a prize crew placed aboard the Norwegian ship. Further inspection revealed that she was equipped with a main transmitter of forty watts, a main receiver and a portable

receiver, a portable engine generator, and a control
panel. She was a well-equipped weather ship used by the
Germans for transmitting weather reports to their units.
The primary function of the radio station was to provide
German U-boats with weather reports, as well as with
information on Allied ships due to pass through the area.

Smith left the *Buskoe* with a prize crew on board and
set out to find the suspected radio station on the east
coast of Greenland. On the following night he anchored
in a fjord about five miles from the approximate location
of the station. Twelve men led by a lieutenant were assigned to attack and capture the radio station. About
midnight the land party proceeded in a small boat to
within a mile of the station. The pitch blackness of the
night and the icy ground made travel very difficult and
hazardous for the landing party. But their efforts were
rewarded by their discovery of the so-called hunter's
shack which had been described to them as the site of
the radio station. The lieutenant threw a cordon of men
around the shack. Then, gun in hand, he kicked in the
door of the building and rushed in on three men who
were resting in their bunks. Taken completely by surprise, the German radiomen surrendered to the lieutenant. They readily told all they knew. Captured with them
were their radio equipment and code. But they were not
without guile. Pretending to make a fire to prepare some
coffee for the Americans, the radiomen tried to burn
some papers. The Coast Guardsmen were too quick for
them and seized the papers. They turned out to contain

149

when she was officially decommissioned. Another epic had ended in which the *Bear* had performed magnificently. In her seventieth year she had taken her place among the ships of the line which had won the Battle of the Atlantic and helped change the course of human history. A historic ship was leaving the scene of world history.

Perhaps the cruelest blow for the *Bear* came one day after D-Day, on June 7, 1944, when the resurgent forces of the Allies made their bid for victory in Europe. On that day the *Bear* was taken off the list of active ships. The conqueror of the Arctic and Antarctic, which had sailed under some of the greatest skippers of her time, had come to the end of a long voyage. She was tied up at Hingham, Massachusetts, with other old ships. It appeared that the fate which had threatened her several times in her long life might have at last caught up with her. This time a reprieve was unlikely.

After the end of World War II the heroic old vessel was turned over to the United States Maritime Commission for sale. In February, 1948, she was sold, less engines and machinery, to the Shaw Steamship Company of Halifax, Nova Scotia. Before purchasing her, the new owners examined the hull and found it still sound and seaworthy. The vessel was towed to Mahone Bay, at Halifax, and plans were made to reconvert the old veteran, after more than three score years, to her original role as a sealing vessel. She was renamed the *Arctic Bear*.

A new diesel engine and machinery were purchased for her.

Unfortunately, before the engine and equipment could be installed, wages went up, and the price of seal oil and skins came down. Work on the vessel was discontinued. Her once gleaming white hull was now painted black; she was little more than a hull, with two short masts and deckhouses topside. Economy rather than disability had laid her up.

10

Rest in Peace

Plans were laid in the late 1950's to secure the *Bear* for a floating exhibit for the San Francisco Maritime Historical Museum, but the plans came to nought.

Then the old vessel was purchased by Alfred N. Johnson of Villanova, Pennsylvania, who intended to use her as a floating restaurant and maritime museum. She would be moored on the Philadelphia waterfront, next to the historic battle cruiser *Olympia*, famed warship of the Spanish-American War which had served as Admiral George Dewey's flagship at the Battle of Manila Bay.

The *Bear's* new owner had her restored as she had been at the height of her great career and before the Navy had converted her into a World War II warship. Three tall masts were set in place. Deckhouses and bridge were modified, and a graceful smokestack was erected. The hull was again painted white. On March 16, 1963, the *Bear* was taken in tow by the tug *Irving Birch* bound for Philadelphia. Masted again, she looked rather proud as she was towed out to sea.

Three days later a furious storm arose in the Atlantic, savagely battering the *Bear's* aged timbers. She had faced worse storms, but always with a crew, and now only two men were standing watch aboard her. Soon she began shipping water rapidly.

Suddenly the towline between the *Bear* and the tug snapped, and the old ship was out of control. The skipper of the *Irving Birch* radioed that the *Bear*, with the two men aboard, was listing badly in heavy seas. Then her foremast collapsed, and she wallowed at the mercy of the sea. The waves were so high that the tug could not launch lifeboats to try to rescue the two aboard her.

A radio cry for help brought the U.S. Coast Guard immediately to the aid of an old comrade. A cutter set her course for the *Bear's* position, and two airplanes and a helicopter took off for the scene. Meanwhile, two Canadian airplanes flew to the spot where the tired old vessel was waging her last fight.

One of the American planes dropped a life raft, to which the *Irving Birch* attached a line and maneuvered the raft downwind to the *Bear*. Luckily the two crew men managed to get aboard the raft.

Under lowering skies the sea grew rougher as the old *Bear* settled lower in the water. At 8:15 P.M., Tuesday, March 19, 1963, when twilight gave way to the dark of

The *Bear* leaving Nova Scotia under tow on March 16, 1963, on her final voyage.

night, at a point 90 miles south of Cape Sable, Nova Scotia, the *Bear* gave up the fight and went under. Time had at last done what snow and ice and gale could not. Her long voyage was over; her great deeds were done.

A stern view of the tired old *Bear* on her last voyage and just before her plunge to the bottom of the stormy North Atlantic. The foremast and the mainmast are broken, and the vessel is listing to starboard.

Bibliography

Books

BIXBY, WILLIAM, *Track of the Bear*. New York, David McKay Co., Inc., 1965.

BYRD, RICHARD E., *Discovery*. New York, G. P. Putnam's Sons, 1935.

———, *Little America*. New York, G. P. Putnam's Sons, 1930.

DAVID, EVAN J., *Our Coast Guard*. New York, D. Appleton-Century Co., Inc., 1937.

FOLEY, ALBERT J., SJ, *Bishop Healy, Beloved Outcast*. New York, Farrar, Straus and Young, 1954.

MORISON, SAMUEL ELIOT, *The Battle of the Atlantic*, Vol. 1. Boston, Little, Brown and Co., 1964.

MOSLEY, HARDWICK, *The Romance of North America*. Boston, Houghton Mifflin Co., 1954.

RAPAPORT, STELLA F., *The Bear—Ship of Many Lives*. New York, Dodd, Mead & Co., 1962.

TUCHMAN, BARBARA, *The Proud Tower*. New York, The Macmillan Co., 1965.

WEAD, FRANK, *Gales, Ice and Men*. New York, Dodd, Mead & Co., 1937.

GOVERNMENT PUBLICATIONS

The Coast Guard at War, Greenland Patrol. A historical monograph prepared by the Historical Section, Headquarters, U.S. Coast Guard. Washington, 1946.

Report of the Cruise of the U.S. Revenue Cutter Bear and the Overland Expedition for the Relief of the Whalers in the Arctic Ocean from November 27, 1897 to September 13, 1898. Washington, D.C., Government Printing Office, 1899.

Reports on the Condition of Seal Life on the Rookeries of the Pribilof Islands. Washington, D.C. Government Printing Office, 1896.

In addition to the above, the *Official Transcript of Testimony Taken at the Investigation into the Conduct of Captain M. A. Healy, of the Revenue Cutter Bear,* two documents dated March, 1890, and February, 1896, which are in the files of the National Archives, Washington, D.C., were studied at considerable length. Reference was also made to the San Francisco *Examiner,* November 17, 1895.

Index

Alaska, 43–116
Alaska Commercial Company, 46
Alaskan Patrol, 43–116
Alert, 32, 35
Aleuts, 45–46
American Missionary Society, 70, 81–83
Amundsen, Roald, 108–9
Antarctic exploration, 119–42
Arctic Bear, 151–52
Arctic exploration, 26, 27–40, 108–9
Arey, Ned, 87
Artisarlook, Charlie, 70, 77 *ff.*
Ash, Francis, 24

Bay of Whales, 123 *ff.,* 137 *ff.*
Bear of Oakland, 120 *ff.*
Belvedere, 75, 88, 91–92
Bering Sea Patrol, 43 *ff.*
Bertholf, Ellsworth P., 69, 85–87, 89, 96
Buskoe, 148–49, 150
Byrd, Richard E., 119–42, 144–45

Call, Dr. Samuel J., 69–96 *passim*
Chandler, William, 32
Charting, 145–46
Cochran, Captain, 101, 106, 108–11, 116
Colwell, John C., 38–39
Connell, Maurice, 39
Conservation, marine, 57–58, 114–15
Construction and refittings, 7–10, 13–15, 32–33, 100–1, 105–6, 120–22, 145, 153–54
Convoy duty, 150
Corwin, 43, 52, 114
Cruzen, Richard, 141

Davis, A. B., 43
Dawe, Charles, 24
Discovery II, 130

Decommissioned, 41–42, 116, 118, 150–51
Denmark, 143 *ff.*
Depression, 119–22
Diamond, Levi, 24
Dog sledding, 71 *ff.*

Edison, Joseph, 39
Emory, William H., Jr., 33 *ff.*
Engelstadt, 86
English, Robert A. J., 122–40 *passim*
Eskimos, 43, 44, 50–66, 78 *ff.,* 114

Fengar, Alvin A., 42
Franklin, Sir John, 28
Freeman, Jesse H., 75, 76, 92
Fur sealing, 44–49, 52–53, 55–58, 115

Gage, Lyman, 68–69
Geer, 146
German shipping menace, 143–50
Gjöa, 108–9
Gold rushes, Alaska, 65–66, 67, 71, 97–100, 102
Graham, Alexander, 13–15, 22–24
Great Britain, 48–49, 53, 55–58
Greely, Lieutenant Adolphus Washington, 26, 27–40
Greenland, 34 *ff.,* 143 *ff.*
Grieve (Walter) and Company, 8, 25

Healy, James Augustine, 51
Healy, Mike, 43, 49–66, 114
Healy, Patrick Francis, 51
Hunniccutt, Miss, 86

Ice, 20, 30, 34 *ff.,* 70–71, 76, 110 *ff.,* 126 *ff.*
Indians 43, 44
International Ice Patrol, 17, 144

Irving Birch, 154

Jackson, Dr. Sheldon, 60–64, 114
Japan, sealing and, 56
Jarvis, David H., 69–96
Johansen, Bendick, 128, 131–32
Johnson, Alfred N., 153

Kalenin, Alexis, 71–73
Katmai Volcano, 101
Kettleson, Dr. A. N., 75, 77, 79
King Edward VII Land, 126–27
King Island, 59, 99
Klondike gold rush, 65–66, 67, 71
Koltchoff, F., 69, 73, 85

Labrador Current, 16–17
Lady Franklin Bay Expedition, 27–40
Launching, 11–13
Law enforcement, 43, 52–53, 64–66
Life Saving Service, 101
Liquor, 44, 45, 58, 66, 104–5
Little America, 123 *ff.*, 137 *ff.*
Loch Garry, 32, 35
Lockwood, James Booth, 38
Long, Francis, 38–39
Lopp, W. T., 81–83, 87–90, 94

Maud, 108–9
McClintock, Sir Francis, 28
McKinley, William, 68
Mercy missions, 98–100, 114
Mikkel, 77
Millard, Captain, 91
Motion pictures, 119
Museum ship, 119–20, 153

Napoleon, 54
Neimo, Peter J., 145
Neptune, 30
Neutrality Patrol, 145–50
New Zealand, 123, 125
Newfoundland, 16 *ff.*
Nome, 97–98, 102
Northland, 112, 116
North Magnetic Pole, 109
North Star, 140
Northwest Passage, 27, 109

Oakland (California), 110, 118–20
Orca, 75, 76, 92, 96

Patrol duty, 43–116, 143–50
Pennell, H. L. L., 136
Pike, Richard, 29
Point Barrow, 69–96 *passim*, 99, 114
Prohibition, 104–5
Proteus, 29, 30, 34, 37, 40

Rae, Sir John, 28
Randall, George M., 74
Reindeer, 60–64, 69–70, 74, 77 *ff.*, 99, 114
Reputation, 96
Rescue operations, 26, 27–40, 43, 54, 68–96, 101, 108–9, 113, 150
Restoration, 153–54
Revenue Cutter Service, 42–101
Roosevelt, Franklin D., 140, 146
Ross, Sir James, 109
Ross Ice Barrier, 136
Ross Sea, 123 *ff.*, 134 *ff.*
Ruppert, Jacob, 120–25, 126, 134, 138, 139
Rush, 43, 49
Russia, 56, 104, 105

St. John's (Newfoundland), 15, 20, 25
St. Michael, 73–75, 102
Samms, Reverend and Mrs. Robert, 86
San Francisco, 43, 110, 112, 116
San Francisco Maritime Historical Museum, 153
Schley, Winfield Scott, 32, 35
Schneider, Roderick R., 39
Scotland, 7–13
Scott, Robert, F., 136
Sea Scouts, 119
Sealing, 15–25, 44–49, 52–53, 55–58, 151–52
Seaworthiness, 13–15, 20, 50, 106–8, 125, 126, 139, 151
Shaw Steamship Company, 151–52
Sherman, Captain, 96
Siberia, 62, 104
Sinking, 154–55
Smith, Edward H., 148–50
Stephen Company, 8–12
Storms, 33, 106–8, 122–23
Submarine patrol, 143–50

159

Teller Reindeer Station, 70, 74, 81, 99
Thetis, 32, 35–38
Thornton, H. R., 64
Tilton, Mr., 75, 93
Treasury Department, 42, 50, 112–14
Tuttle, Francis, 66, 67–71, 96

Ubberroth, Preston H., 104
United States Antarctic Service, 140
United States Coast Guard, 42, 144–50, 101 ff., 154
United States Navy, 26, 32 ff., 41, 42

Vincent, J. B., 54

Waesche, Russell R., 144–45
Weather observation posts, polar, 29
Weather patrol, 150
Weyprecht, Karl, 28–29
Whalers, 66, 67, 87 ff., 102, 110
Wilkins, Sir Hubert, 116
World War I, 101
World War II, 143–51

Young Phoenix, 53–54
Yukon gold rush, 97–100

The Authors

Robert H. Rankin, a retired U.S. Marine Corps colonel, has published many articles and books on aviation and military and naval history. Born in Martins Ferry, Ohio, he is a graduate of Eastern Kentucky State College. Before serving with the Marines he was both an enlisted man and officer in the U.S. Army. He lives in Falls Church, Virginia.

H. R. Kaplan, a resident of Washington, D.C., has been writing professionally for nearly thirty years. His articles have appeared in a great variety of magazines, and this is his third book. He was a lawyer and a teacher before he devoted his full time to writing.